A Market Stoi ..
Newcastle-under-Lyme

a history of 'on the stones'

Paul Anderton

First Printing, 2023

Published by Clayhanger Press
7 Highfield Court
Newcastle under Lyme
Staffordshire
ST5 3LT
www.clayhangerpress.co.uk

ISBN-13: 978-1-7391770-7-2

Contents

Foreword

There has been a market in Newcastle-under-Lyme for 850 years, ever since the right to hold one was granted by the royal charter conferred on the settlement in the year 1173 by King Henry II.

Like a thread woven through our history, the market in the centre of our town has been a presence through the centuries; shoppers and traders enjoying bumper harvests or dealing with crop failures, or facing the impact of land enclosures and the industrial revolution, all the while a constant event as monarchs change, empires pass and technology changes society.

Newcastle-under-Lyme's long and varied history is particularly on my mind at present, as we celebrate our 850th anniversary as a Borough.

I can trace my family's presence in Newcastle-under-Lyme as far back as 1721. That's a generation before the second Jacobite rebellion marched south to the Midlands, more than a century before Queen Victoria came to the throne and two hundred years before one of our greatest sons, R.J. Mitchell, who designed the Spitfire, was born in Butt Lane. Philip Astley, widely acknowledged as the 'father of the modern circus' was born just a stones throw from the Market in 1742, while Silverdale - born Sir Joseph Cook - worked in the mines as a nine-year-old before following a path which would lead in 1913 to the office of Prime Minister of Australia. Remarkable people, remarkable achievements and it's remarkable to think that they and my own ancestors would all be familiar with our market, its stalls and atmosphere.

This book explores our shared past, but by focusing on something that stands the test of time I think it is a celebration of our future too.

Cllr Simon Tagg
Leader Newcastle-under-Lyme Borough Council
July 2023.

One

Setting the scene

Every Monday Nick Moore walks the streets of Newcastle-under-Lyme. He goes along Ironmarket and turns into High Street to join clusters of people gathered in the town's market. Stalls with strikingly patterned covers line a street which for 850 years at least has been the site for traders to meet customers. Nick is the latest in a long line of collectors of stall rents, once known as tolls, but has far wider responsibilities than ever his predecessors had. He manages the use and development of the High Street for Newcastle-under-Lyme Borough Council. He plans events aimed at drawing in visitors with money to spend. A market is a magnet. It attracts and entertains. Buying and selling there is a person-to-person exchange, an increasingly rare experience. The more people crowd in, the more colourful and varied the stalls, the more lively the traders touting their wares, the better for the town's businesses as a whole. Life, vibrancy, action make for success. Known to locals as 'on the stones' this street as an open-air and all-weather shopping venue makes Newcastle distinctive in North Staffordshire's urban landscape.

For the borough of Newcastle the market is a prize asset, as it has been for centuries. Today more than ever it is actively promoted as a public investment. New traders are positively encouraged to lease stalls and customers are enticed to spend time browsing the widest range of goods. 'Footfall' is the magic measure of success, the number of stalls in use at any one time a vital statistic. A market is not a spontaneous event, but a managed facility carefully arranged by an officer of the borough.

Nor is it a once-a-week activity. On different days the stalls are leased to specific types of traders. On Mondays and Fridays a general market is held according to a centuries old tradition. Older local people talk about Roy Aslett as one of the prominent traders, and recall with affection his shirt and tie stall. Len White still has a fruit and vegetable stall where his wife, and son Steven, work. The Whites are a Newcastle family trading on the stones for a hundred years. Jean proudly talks of the time her predecessors came in using a horse and cart. Unfortunately, there are fewer family businesses, career traders one might say, now working only in a market.

In conjunction with the National Market Trader Federation (NMTF) one of the innovations at Newcastle is a day set aside for young or new traders to try their luck in retailing in the hope that this will start a long career. Special terms, including token rents for an initial period, are attractive inducements. This encourages traders aged between 16 and 30 into the retail industry and showcases enterprising and creative young people who are starting up. Market stalls are ideal launch pads for young businesses where costs and overheads are low. Young traders can enter a national competition, The NMTF Young Traders Market Initiative. In 2022 Abigail Proctor of "Abi Through the Ears" progressed from the regional to the National Finals in Stratford-Upon-Avon and was placed fourth overall.

There are enterprising young people who have brought new life into Newcastle's market on a longer-term basis. Liam and George Smith ensure that a business their father Alan built up did not fold when the covid epidemic hit Britain in 2020. Fish from Fleetwood is their speciality. Alan had a stall for over twenty years in Newcastle which is now a compact refrigerated van with stylish awning plentifully stocked with seafood fresh from the dockside in Lancashire. Liam and

Figure 1: Liam and George Smith with fish from Fleetwood

George start their day around 4.00am collecting locally caught fish and Scottish as well as Cornish produce. On the way to Sandbach on a Thursday and Newcastle on a Friday they deliver to shops in Manchester. They set out their wares whatever the weather and pack up about 2.00pm to start the trek home. Enroute they may deliver to Stoke City Football

Club and some private clients. Between carefully gutting and dressing whole fish as customers require, both Liam and George greet old faces and new people with refreshingly engaging chatter. Service with a laugh, the pleasure of market trading exemplified. New to the life of a market trader is Jonathan Hill. Graphic designing gave him a career, but the need he felt was to run a café. He made the change just before the covid crisis in the long tradition of would-be business owners. By taking a market pitch and renovating a van, he opened his coffee stall using a couple of chairs at the

side for customers. Conditions when covid restrictions on travel and shopping eased brought people out looking for open-air shopping. A cup of fresh, high quality coffee with a little

Figure 2: Jonathan Hill serving coffee

something to bite on, sheltered beneath Jonathan's gazebo, was very welcome. Most days of the week Jonathan, now with his son Ben, makes the short trip from his Newcastle home to his place near the Guildhall. Maybe he will achieve his ambition of permanent premises one day, but in the meantime he has plans to extend his range of foods on offer from his cleverly converted horsebox.

More experienced, and perhaps a touch more pessimistic, is Darren Taylor. He is easy to talk to at his plant stall set up three times a week, having supplied a large variety of allotment and garden plants to discerning customers for over twenty years. Two days he spends collecting his goods from a

Figure 3: Darren Taylor

network of small nurseries from as far away as Wem in Shropshire. Darren has memories of the days when traders arrived at 6.00am practically fighting to get a stall, and when the waiting list he joined was almost six months long. The tasks of setting up were laborious. Young lads looking for a few shillings started early for school and did fetching and carrying. As a local boy himself, who spent twenty-five years employed in industry, and now living in Penkhull, Darren Taylor has witnessed significant changes in the circumstances in which trading has been done 'on the stones'. His first pitch was at the lower end of High Street. His aim was to qualify for a space more or less where he is now. Darren explains with some vigour how he achieved his ambition.

On the third Sunday of each month and soon to celebrate its second birthday, an Artisan Market goes from strength to strength. Occupied by traders from a 15 mile radius, every one of the 45 fixed stalls is consistently taken by fledgling businesses, home-based artisan producers and charities. The market pitch areas are fully used from the southern end of the market to the Guildhall with entertainment being just one attraction.

Figure 4: Happy shoppers and stalls on a recent market day

Additional pop-up stalls have been hired which have enabled up to 70 traders to come to recent markets. A most pleasing aspect to the popularity of Castle Artisan Market is that some Newcastle-under-Lyme businesses have opted to take a stall, in addition to their permanent premises. This expands their sales and revives an ancient tradition.

Figure 5 Town Crier

Other special interests catered for at different markets are those of dog lovers, record enthusiasts, devotees of vegan cuisine and hunters of antiques. Such a mix of events, having electricity for power and lighting laid on, as well as employing a borough council officer to find and negotiate with new and established traders, are characteristics of a managed market.

Since 2019, Newcastle Borough Council, as owner of the market rights, has adopted a much more proactive role than was formerly the case.

It never has been a free-for-all, or accidental feature of an ancient town. There has been a degree of supervision required from the start. When was that start, and how were markets run in times past? What significant changes have been made in the past which help to explain how the market has arrived at its current position? A medieval charter still applicable today established its legal status. Not that this and the circumstances of its production and subsequent revisions are examined here. That's a story for another time.

One change easily identified took place in 1835, and that is taken here as a convenient starting point for a story of Newcastle's market. In effect, control over the market passed from a privileged, narrowly defined and very self-interested group, to a public authority with significant consequences. Of course, many influences thereafter affected the market, notably alterations in the wider world of retail shopping. This is not the place to recount, for example, the history of the town's numerous greengrocers, drapers, ironmongers, butchers, bakers and pharmacies. Much could be written about how department and chain stores came to flourish and disappear. What matters for the present is that, despite substantial competition even in the age of the supermarket, Newcastle's street market survives. There is a story here worth telling.

It has to be noted also that markets are features of human history of greater significance than just the one in Newcastle. Our understanding of markets as the term is currently used, is primarily based on what we see 'on the stones', though that may not be the whole story.

Two   **Newcastle-under-Lyme:**
                           a market evolves

In its ancient form a market is easy to understand. It is in a simple sense one of civilization's foundation stones. People in towns had limited space and yet needed to buy food brought in by rural producers. Country folk had to sell surplus animals and crops for cash to buy goods made in towns, and pay taxes. Circumstances change and markets change with them. Markets still held in Newcastle on Mondays in 2022 had stalls set out along High Street (previously known as Penkhull Street), lining what was the main routeway to London until about 1965. They are a remnant of an institution located in a town which in 2023 celebrates being at least 850 years old.

Figure 6: A market day 2023

In a space in the shadow of a newly built castle, long before the market's first specific record in 1203,[1] people almost certainly congregated to sell produce using temporary structures to display their wares. Buyers from anywhere walked around choosing whatever they needed. Probably from the beginning, those who had live animals to sell required space to pen or tie them, though the effectiveness of restraints varied enormously. Cattle were herded into and out of market areas, usually disrupting and befouling lines of stalls displaying butter, cheese, eggs and all other manner of foodstuffs, textiles, iron and pottery ware. One street, long called Ironmarket, suggests it had a specialised role at least for a time. All the while, Newcastle as a town evolved.

Figure 7: A decorative feature of the borough charter issued by James II in 1686

In the absence of evidence to the contrary, it has to be assumed that the weekly gathering of traders and buyers in Newcastle was controlled and regulated much like markets elsewhere. Authority lay with the burgesses under the remit of a borough charter originally granted in 1173 and renewed several times in the seventeenth century. In addition to whatever byelaws were laid down locally, a few royal edicts and the'occasional Parliamentary Act supplied the rules, but policing was a matter for the borough's burgesses to arrange.

The operation of a street market where buyers met producers in person was a defining activity for a particular kind of society – a pre-industrial society described by some historians as having a 'moral economy'. This was one where 'what is right' was considered to be the best test of good trading: and wrongdoing was that action which caused goods to be bought and sold in a manner detrimental to the community as a whole. For example, an Act under Charles II allowed customers, in the case of wheat and similar goods measured in bushel containers, to shake the standardised vessel to ensure that they had full value!

Figure 8: Imperial standard bushel
measure held in Brampton Museum

An early eighteenth-century handbook advising parish and borough constables about laws they were supposed to enforce, explained that certain trading practices were punishable as being against the interest of consumers. It stated that *"Forestallers of Markets, and Ingrossers and Regrators are punishable by Justices of the Peace in their Quarter Sessions, on the presentment of Constables."* In effect, middlemen who sought to operate in the space between the producer and the consumer were acting against the public interest, as they tended to push up the price of goods, especially food. In the words of the book, *"And a Forestaller by Statute is declared to be one who buys Victuals, or Merchandize, etc, by the Way, before it is brought to a Fair or Market, to the intent to sell the same at a higher price;*

A Regrator is one that buys any grain, butter, cheese etc in a Fair or Market, and sells the same in the same Market, or within four miles:

and an Ingrosser is one who buys corn growing etc, or butter or cheese, with an intent to sell again. Stat. 5 & 6 Ed.6. c 14."

If found guilty the miscreants were liable to prison, fines and humiliation.

"These offenders shall forfeit for the first offence the value of the goods, and suffer two months imprisonment; and for the second offence double the penalty etc; and for the third offence shall lose all their goods, and be set in the pillory etc.

But maltsters buying barley, Badgers of Corn, Butchers, and Poulterers etc are excepted out of the Act."

It would be necessary to undertake a more tightly focused study of Newcastle's early borough records than is done here, in order to discover how effectively the burgesses enforced market regulations before the nineteenth century. The suspicion is that control was relaxed long before Queen Victoria came to the throne and that middlemen, for example, operated more or less unhindered as the country as a whole began to move into a period of commercial and industrial revolution.

Extracts from a guide book used by parish officials to advise them on the law that they were obliged to enforce.

At a Hay-Market — "For carts of hay which stand to be sold in the Hay-Market, so much per load is to be paid towards the paving and amending the street; and they shall not stand laden after 3 o'clock in the afternoon etc under penalty of 5s. And persons selling trusses of hay wanting due weight, shall forfeit for every truss 2s-6d to be levied by Constables, by warrant of a justice.

Stat. 2 W & M. cap 8

there is to be one measure etc throughout the kingdom

Magn. Chart. 9.H.3

every city, borough, town is to have a common ballance to weigh goods bought and sold, with common weights sealed, in the keeping of the Head Officer or Constable there; otherwise the City forfeits £10; the borough £4, and the town 40s.

Stat. 8 H. 6c. 5

at this ballance all the inhabitants of the said city ..... may weigh gratis, but foreigners shall for every draught under forty pounds, pay a farthing; for a draught between forty pounds and one hundred an half-penny, and above one hundred pounds a penny

Stat. ibid

mayors shall view all measures and weights once a year, break or burn those which are defective

persons selling corn or salt by any bushell or measure not according to standard, and struck even with the brim, shall forfeit 40s

Over time, conventions and practices in many similar English market towns separated out goods for sale into different markets, sometimes held on different days and in different spaces. Permanent retail shops evolved, and in the nineteenth century large emporia were established, but they did not undermine or replace markets.

By Victorian times there was greater public awareness of the advantages of more effective market regulation and more convenient locations. So, for example, in Newcastle in 1853 a Covered Market was built in Penkhull Street (High Street now) to accommodate traders in perishable foods. In 1871 cattle selling was removed to a purpose-built arena some distance from streets used as an open market site. These are the simple, anodyne statements in a volume of the *Victoria History of Staffordshire*[2]. It was not, however, quite so simple or as inevitable as this factual listing in an orthodox history presents.

Three   Newcastle market in a changing economy

First of all, these simple statements underplay the significance to the chartered borough of its market. Particularly after the castle lost its purpose, Newcastle's economic and social function was as a market town. For centuries it provided the only legal meeting place for buyers and sellers in a large agricultural area. A survey in 1516 found 50 markets in the county and the nearest to Newcastle were at Madeley, Betley and Talke. A little further away Stone, Eccleshall and Leek had markets. Today, Leek, Stone, Stafford, Market Drayton, Sandbach and Nantwich are its nearest open-air rivals.

Within Newcastle's immediate neighbouring district five settlements at Tunstall, Burslem, Hanley, Stoke and Longton, from the mid-eighteenth century, grew to become substantial industrial communities and all were prevented from having markets by Newcastle's monopoly rights. In these Potteries towns markets only emerged late. Hanley's inhabitants built a market house in 1776 from voluntary subscriptions, but could not allow trading in corn.[3] Burslem employed a subterfuge in 1761 to hide an intention to have a market hall. These moves were much to the annoyance of traders in the ancient borough. Those who opened up permanent shops in Newcastle recognised that though itinerant stall holders were to some extent competitors, they also attracted crowds on market days just as likely to patronise grocers, druggists, bakers and bookshops as out-of-doors egg and butter sellers. Those bringing animals for sale were even more welcome as they drank in the pubs, did deals there, ate and socialised, all the more so if they had made good money early in the day. To that end it was in every trader's interest that the market attracted high quality animals of many kinds; fat cattle, strong cart horses and heavy sheep especially.

NEWCASTLE-UNDER-LYME

Is a *Borough*, *Market-town*, and *Parish*, comprising within its limits 607 acres of land, and a population which, since the year 1801, has increased from 4604 to 8192 souls, of whom 3831 are males, and 4361 females. It is pleasantly seated on a small stream that flows southward to the Trent, 1¼ mile W. of Stoke, in the Potteries; 16 miles N.N.W. of Stafford, 12 miles S. W. by W. of Leek, and 151 miles N. W. by W. of London. The town is generally well-built, and most of the streets are remarkably wide and well paved; and being on the direct road from Liverpool and Manchester to London and Birmingham, it is a great thoroughfare for coaches, carriers, and travellers of every description. It enjoys the benefit of a canal from the coal-mines, near Audley, to the Trent and Mersey canal, near Stoke, and has long been famous for the manufacture of *hats*, which gives employment to a considerable number of the inhabitants. Here are also two large *silk-mills*, and an extensive *cotton* manufactory. Monday is the chartered *Market-day* for corn, &c.; but another market on Saturday was established about twenty years ago, to meet the demands of the increased population, and it is now the principal market for flesh, vegetables, &c. Here are also five annual FAIRS for horses, cattle, woollen cloth, and other merchandise, held on Shrove-Monday, Easter-Monday, Whit-Monday, the first Monday in November, and on the first Mondays after July 15th and Sept. 11th. The *wake*, or feast, is on the Sunday before St. Giles's day; and the *Horse-Races* are held about the middle of July, on *Knutton Heath*, near the north-west side of the town.

Figure 9: From White's Directory and Gazetteer of Staffordshire 1834

Secondly, merely to only state that a Covered Market and new cattle market site were established, is to ignore the problematic circumstances which did not make them inevitable actions. By the middle of the nineteenth century it was clear that the role of 'capital of the Potteries' no longer applied to Newcastle. As a base for industrial wealth it had never achieved anything worthwhile despite manufacturing smokers' clay pipes and beaver hats. Its banking and professional services, medical expertise and assembly rooms were increasingly duplicated in Burslem and Hanley. It lost its status as a post office hub and with the arrival of railways had but secondary importance to Whitmore (station 1837) and then Stoke (station 1849) as a link to the wider world. Moreover, its local reputation was somewhat sullied by association with political corruption, at both Parliamentary and municipal level. This was not entirely forgotten despite reforms in the 1830s. In this context, weekly markets and several annual fairs were of ever greater economic value to Newcastle, to be guarded and preserved for the money and vibrancy they brought to the commercial heart of the borough.

Moreover, one particular section of the market, that for selling cattle, had been hard hit by a national disaster. This was a rinderpest epidemic, or cattle plague, lasting from June 1865 to October 1867. For many months the borough council forbade the admission of cattle into the town as a method of preventing the spread of disease. Cheshire was the worst hit county, but large numbers of Staffordshire animals were slaughtered to assist in disease eradication.[4] Cattle were brought back to Newcastle in November 1867 and this may have created a demand for new arrangements for their place of sale.[5]

In the third place, the simple statements of the Victoria County History fail to indicate the effect of an external force on Newcastle's system of government, and hence the management of its market.

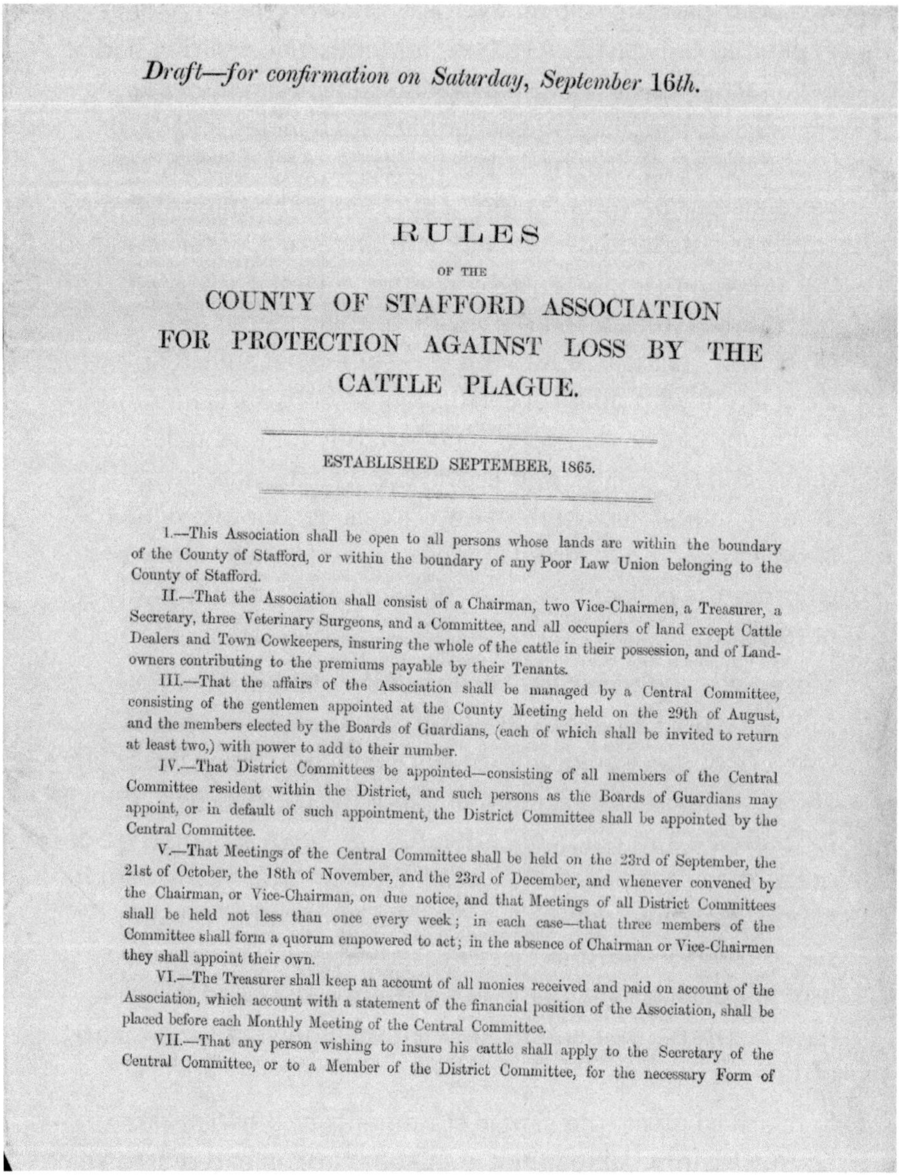

RULES

OF THE

COUNTY OF STAFFORD ASSOCIATION
FOR PROTECTION AGAINST LOSS BY THE
CATTLE PLAGUE.

ESTABLISHED SEPTEMBER, 1865.

I.—This Association shall be open to all persons whose lands are within the boundary of the County of Stafford, or within the boundary of any Poor Law Union belonging to the County of Stafford.

II.—That the Association shall consist of a Chairman, two Vice-Chairmen, a Treasurer, a Secretary, three Veterinary Surgeons, and a Committee, and all occupiers of land except Cattle Dealers and Town Cowkeepers, insuring the whole of the cattle in their possession, and of Land-owners contributing to the premiums payable by their Tenants.

III.—That the affairs of the Association shall be managed by a Central Committee, consisting of the gentlemen appointed at the County Meeting held on the 29th of August, and the members elected by the Boards of Guardians, (each of which shall be invited to return at least two,) with power to add to their number.

IV.—That District Committees be appointed—consisting of all members of the Central Committee resident within the District, and such persons as the Boards of Guardians may appoint, or in default of such appointment, the District Committee shall be appointed by the Central Committee.

V.—That Meetings of the Central Committee shall be held on the 23rd of September, the 21st of October, the 18th of November, and the 23rd of December, and whenever convened by the Chairman, or Vice-Chairman, on due notice, and that Meetings of all District Committees shall be held not less than once every week; in each case—that three members of the Committee shall form a quorum empowered to act; in the absence of Chairman or Vice-Chairmen they shall appoint their own.

VI.—The Treasurer shall keep an account of all monies received and paid on account of the Association, which account with a statement of the financial position of the Association, shall be placed before each Monthly Meeting of the Central Committee.

VII.—That any person wishing to insure his cattle shall apply to the Secretary of the Central Committee, or to a Member of the District Committee, for the necessary Form of

Figure 10: The cattle plague of 1865 in Staffordshire

Four   Newcastle's new form of government and divisions of opinion

Conditions were exactly right, in other words, around the time Victoria became Queen, for dissention and controversy. A community in the doldrums is prone to fall apart as some see scope for improvement, seek remedies for perceived inadequacies and promote plans which require monetary expenditure. They come up against preservers, defenders of established practices, and a reluctance to support anything which requires public money – taxes – to pay for schemes altering entrenched modes of living and working.

In the case of Newcastle another circumstance, quite outside the control of its inhabitants, profoundly altered the arena in which decision-making took place. In 1835, under the Municipal Corporations Act, the borough had to adopt a new governing body. This piece of Parliamentary legislation was but one element in a set of reforms of government at local and national level implemented by a political party later called Liberal. In effect, the former closed system of borough governance based on the privileged rights of burgesses was opened up with an injection of democracy. All ratepayers now had a vote in the election of 18 councillors. The town's governing body, in other words, represented 1,700 householders, not 532 men with burgess qualifications.[6]

Councillors each served for three years and required re-election to continue in office. Six of them were elevated to the status of aldermen (six years in office) and were replaced as councillors at by-elections. This new Borough Council inherited the assets and responsibilities of the previous regime, including control of the market. The story of how the major alterations in market trading were made in 1853 and 1871 may be best explained by starting in 1835.

Figure 11: Newcastle market place by J. A. Hammersley 1843

Newcastle's first councillors elected by the ratepayers faced an immediate demand to build a Covered Market to improve the conditions under which market traders operated. It seems that this ambition was one blocked by the previous burgess-controlled Corporation, though for how long is uncertain. Public expenditure was required, and not welcomed. The capital cost and running charges were expected to fall on market traders who paid a fee or toll to set up a stall. Burgesses claimed the right to trade toll free, but this was not likely to be possible if a Covered Market had to be lit by gas and needed repair. On the other hand, Newcastle's position as a market centre was under threat from rivals in Potteries towns, and sheltered accommodation was attractive to many food sellers and their customers.

Figure 12: Butcher's Market in Hanley opened in 1831– seen here in 1978

It was in this context that Dr Thomas Mackenzie, newly elected councillor, proposed building a Covered Market. He led the 'improvers', self-advertised in advance of the 1835 election as 'Reformers'. This was their first action.[7] Few could have anticipated the time it took for their hopes to be fulfilled. Anyone farsighted could have predicted a hard fight as the overall complexion of the new Council was judged to be 'Conservative'.[8]

Mackenzie was House Physician at the North Staffordshire Infirmary located at Etruria.[9] He took this appointment at a charity hospital in 1831 as an honorary position because it had advantages for him as a private practitioner, as well as enabling him to establish a public role in the ruling circles of figures dominant in the industrial communities of the area. He seems to have become physician to the Duke of Sutherland's family when present at Trentham.[10] Mackenzie lived on Stubbs Street when elected in 1835 and it is highly unlikely that he was a burgess. He married a local girl and they had their first child in 1821, followed by five others before 1835, all born in Staffordshire. Mackenzie's status and lifestyle was displayed in the 1841 census return which showed four servants, a tutor and a governess in the household. The question which is not easily answered is why he was concerned about the conditions in which market trading took place.

At the close of the new Council's first effective business meeting in February 1836, Mackenzie succeeded in getting a Market Committee appointed to consider the matter of a new building. He was reported as saying that he was moved by a request from numerous butchers to have a Covered Market erected, which he thought might also be useful to dealers in other goods. He suggested that this was a long wished for change, but gave no specific reasons for it, or explanation of why it had not happened before.[11]

Given that in March Mackenzie had a detailed plan to offer the Council, it might be concluded that some individuals had worked on this scheme for some time.[12] It was argued that the necessity for sheltered premises was to keep up with neighbouring towns already provided with indoor markets. The financial calculation was that if tolls were raised to the level of those in other towns, the construction charges, running costs, interest on the necessary loan and the repayment of that loan could all be covered in reasonable time.

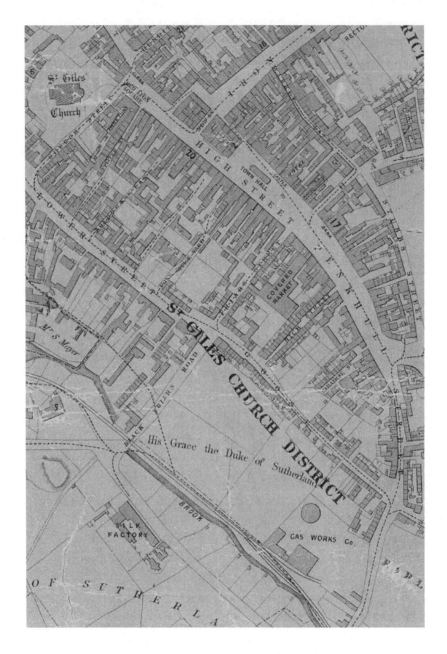

Figure 13: Part of Robert Malabar's map of Newcastle circa 1856

Several sites had been examined and surveyed by an architect. Indeed, Mr Chapman had worked out that 180 stalls and 112 places for women selling butter could be provided. In effect, the aim was to put all traders under one roof. Nothing was said, however, about those selling live animals.

All in all, between £6,000 and £7,000 would be needed and could be satisfactorily managed. Mackenzie's plan was based upon a current toll income of about £430, increased to nearer £1,000 per year when new conditions were in operation. A large majority approved the plan for a general Covered Market in principle before the suitability of several sites was debated. Then the divisions of opinion surfaced.

Five places were put forward, and narrowed by vote to three. Two were in High Street and the third in Merrial Street. A final choice was deferred until more was known about purchase prices. The ground areas varied between 1,600 and 2,100 square yards approximately, or about 40 yards long and 50 yards wide on the larger site. A tight squeeze for nearly 300 traders! How close this was to matching the numbers who actually set up every week along High Street is anyone's guess.

In further council meetings an opposition to the market project became more evident. Mackenzie reported that the site with the lowest purchase price was in the Friar's Lane area, with the Crown Inn and part of a bowling green behind liable to be replaced. However, 250 residents signed a petition against the plan, including the occupants of three principal inns. Three quarters of the town's tradesmen, it was claimed, were signatories. Criticism focused on the notion of a general market as opposed to some improved premises for butchers. What was suggested was that a Shambles for meat sellers might be acceptable, but not the end of outdoor trading for all other goods. In any case, the Friar's Lane site, although the favoured one for the Reformers, was too far from the commercial centre of the town, and from the eastern part of the town where some new building was expected. Although not overtly reported, it appears that the proposed High Street plot was on a steep slope and presented some difficulties for older people. Perhaps the real objection was from burgesses, who feared that they would lose their privilege of trading in the streets toll free. Councillor Hall stated this openly.[13]

Judging by the way the council meeting was reported, Mackenzie was scornful of his opponents arguments and questioned their motives, to their obvious annoyance. He failed to defeat a motion to reverse the adoption of a general market by two votes - ten to eight with two abstentions and six absentees.[14] In November Mackenzie lost his seat at the elections. Clearly, he was identified as an enemy of burgesses, despite his strenuous denials.[15]

1847: a second plan for a Covered Market

In 1847 the matter of improving market facilities emerged again when T. W. Mayer and Dr Mackenzie were among a group keen to build a Covered Market space. Towards the end of February they presented the Council with a memorial signed by over 300 individuals calling for a Covered Market. The signatories were said to be nearly all the principal house holders and numerous influential persons in the neighbourhood. At the same time the burgesses made their objections clear. At the subsequent Council meeting Mayer argued that tolls collected from traders could be raised from £400 to £700 per annum, but of the £6,000 required £1,000 need not be borrowed. It was a long meeting, perhaps somewhat heated, as burgesses expressed the fear that they might lose the right to put up stalls toll free. The source of loans was also controversial. In the end, key decisions to acquire a site were unanimously agreed. One in High Street mostly owned by Sir F. F. Boughey was suggested, but owners of other property were to be invited to submit alternatives. Apparently, a consequence would be the shift of the potato traders to a place near the Cross, whereas there was no clear plan for a hay and straw market. Corn would be traded in the Town Hall on Mondays. The sop to the burgesses was that a small section of a Covered Market would be reserved for their use, provided they contributed to the cost of gas lighting.[16]

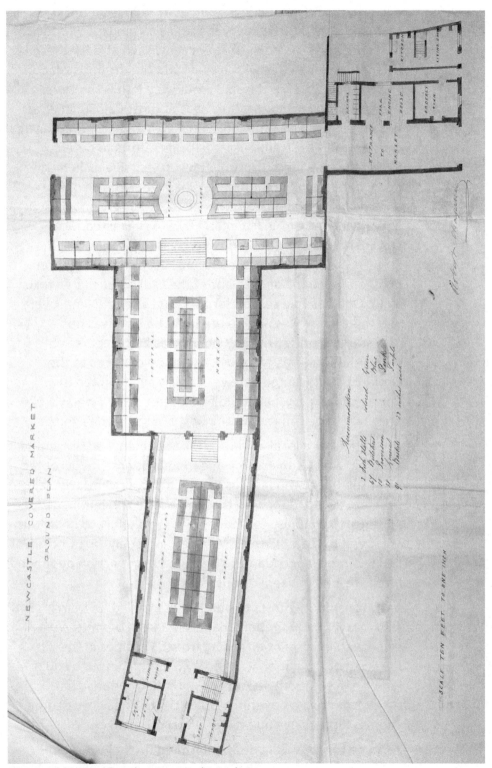

Figure 14: Plan for the Covered Market

29

Despite the decisions in March, arguments, if not deliberate delaying tactics, resumed in April with a focus on the location of the Covered Market. Mayer and his committee wanted to purchase a site in Penkhull Street (now High Street) offered by Thomas Kinnersley with a small addition from Dr Wood. The purchase cost of this and a roadway into Friars Lane, *"opposite the Railway Station"* was at most £2,000. In effect, this was the same Castle Inn proposal of 1836. Dr Mackenzie was reported as strenuously opposing efforts to defer decisions as he feared another eleven years delay in much needed market improvements. Clearly, the choice of site allowed his opponents the chance to use diversionary tactics, and other locations in Ironmarket were suggested for consideration. The vote, however, was in favour of High Street 13 to 1 with four abstentions, despite fears that only butchers would be able to afford the likely rent charge for stalls. One possible reason for the success of the 'improvers' was that Mayer was able to argue that a loan was not necessarily required as the Council was in the course of selling the former Workhouse and some cottages to the Orme Trust. It wanted a new school, Mayer wanted a Covered Market. What could be a better deal? Finally, a £20 prize was to be offered for the best architect's design.[17]

By September a local architect, Mr Chapman, had presented a design, which subject to some modifications was accepted. An Assurance Company was in negotiations, Mr Mayer said, probably able to supply all the loan necessary, but he needed approval to continue to act. There was an effort to delay this, but it was defeated 7 to 4. However, although the principle of taking out only one loan was agreed, further action depended on the results of negotiations.[18]

As it turned out, efforts to obtain a loan failed. In March 1848 T. W. Mayer had to report that his Market Committee was faced with uncertainties arising from difficulties in the financing of the national economy, and the borough could not offer a sufficient security to potential lenders. The scheme to build a Covered Market on the sites provided by Thomas Kinnersley and Dr Wood was dropped.[19]

To some this was a big disappointment. In the wider world, 1848 was a year of serious disruption considered in certain respects to be revolutionary. For Newcastle, it was a moment when the town fell further behind its nearest neighbours in the Potteries, where Covered Markets busily competed alongside very active animal markets. An inquisitive newspaper reporter in 1850 found Newcastle *"the seat of a dying - almost dead trade – that of the manufacture of beaver hats."* He noted *"men with aprons, having the appearance of operatives in some textile branch of industry, lounging listlessly about the street corners"*. Not the best of publicity.[20]

To cover or not cover market traders was one question dealt with, but another aspect of market management was also controversial. How far the two matters were linked is uncertain but burgess rights were affected in both cases. In simple terms, the Market Inspector, Thomas Cottrill, informed the Borough Council just over four months after the Covered Market project was dropped, that burgesses were occupying too much space in the streets on market days. This prevented farmers and other outside traders from pitching up to the disadvantage of customers. Indeed, in the course of one recent day, the price of potatoes had doubled from one penny a pound to two pence all because only one class of dealer found space. In effect, a monopoly was created. During discussion, it was accepted that the Council had to take care not to infringe burgess rights, but its duty was to see that poorer buyers were not disadvantaged. Cottrill was meticulous in giving evidence. In July he had measured two burgess stalls which he considered excessive at 13 feet by 12 feet, and 13 feet by 8 feet. Two others were 11 feet square.[21] This was not surprising as Cottrill was also Chief Constable!

The reaction of the burgesses to this account of their trading practices by a borough employee is another story in the politics of Newcastle's governing body. A printed report of a sub-committee's recommendation for new market regulations has not survived.

Another external influence

Newcastle was not disconnected from a wider society and economy, and like all other towns was subject to the impact of events originating far away. In 1848 and 1849 a cholera epidemic swept through England. Inquiries into the state of health and the causes of infectious diseases had been taken more seriously since a cholera scare in 1832. Newcastle's councillors ought to have been made aware of the vulnerability of their town to disease, when they answered a questionnaire in 1844 distributed by a Commission of Inquiry into the State of Large Towns and Populous Districts. They acknowledged then that in many parts of the town filth, household rubbish and commercial waste, was simply emptied out into the streets to putrify in a most unpleasant manner. In courts and alleys *"the refuse and filth is carted off at the capricious pleasure of the occupants or landlords"*. Fresh water supplies were not available in many working-class homes, but came from standpipes and wells. The town had no public baths *"but there are every facilities for public bathing in our canals, without a nuisance."* An air of complacency was conveyed by the collective response to 62 quite searching questions.[22]

In 1849 a more thorough inspection by a government agent into public health conditions in Newcastle took place deserving more attention than possible here. It was required as the death rate, at 28 per thousand in the population, greatly exceeded a norm laid down in recent Public Health legislation. Suffice it to say that the report of William Lee describing health hazards overshadowing the town's inhabitants, was an encouragement to 'improvers' to press more vigorously than ever for projects for public benefit. Not that Lee, or the 1844 inquiry for that matter, examined the markets or food selling as contributors to a high death rate. Lee was strongly of the opinion, however, that there were no natural reasons for the high incidence of disease, only human neglect and failure to invest in appropriate infrastructure. A new cemetery, a proper water borne sewage system and effective removal of detritus from homes and streets were among his principal recommendations. Once again, therefore, external forces were shaping Newcastle's development.

For whatever reasons, in 1852 to '54 the council chose to prioritise two improvements in the wake of Lee's inquiry of 1849. A public Bath House was opened in May 1852 in School Street to provide a washing facility most of the town's inhabitants did not possess at home. Two plunge baths, each ten yards long, and several bath tubs for individual use were available to both sexes, and there were washing and drying facilities for clothes. Perhaps there was some recognition here that access to canals for bathing, as reported in 1844, was hardly a satisfactory way of keeping working people clean.

Less obviously a response to Lee's conclusions about public heath was the other action. Within months a second project, a Covered Market, was launched no longer involving Dr Mackenzie. This was a more ambitious building and public facility intended to cater for the needs of small retailers. It also effectively divided the established market, separating out animal sales which remained an open-air activity. It is not clear how farmers and auctioneers responded to this and whether any of them began looking for public assistance to improve their trading conditions.

Financing the Covered Market project required a loan and central government permission to raise £5,000. This was approved at a rate of 4¼ percent. Mr Chapman drew up preliminary plans, but these did not cover all the ground which the council bought. Additions were therefore discussed in April 1853 amounting to a new police station and cells, with a court room, living quarters for a police superintendent, housing for a fire engine and a pig and sheep market. There was also a request for storage space for equipment and ammunition used by a militia unit, together with two rooms for the use of its non-commissioned officers. Councillors Turner and Cartwright presented these proposals and obtained unanimous support. Staffordshire magistrates were delighted with the offer to their militia regiment.[23]

The following month the council heard that its Markets and Tolls Committee had negotiated the purchase of the Crown Inn, Penkhull Street, for £1,200 and additional land from a Dr Wood and the Duke of Sutherland, subject to contract and council approval. There was a complication in the deal involving the tenant of the Crown who had bought an adjacent property to convert to a pub on his departure from the inn. He wanted a right of way across the Covered Market site to allow access from Penkhull Street to his proposed hostelry. This was refused.[24]

Tenders from builders were expected to be in by 2 July for what was, in effect, a major investment in three public services; police, militia and market.[25] Surviving plans by Robert Chapman do not show any provision for a police force or a pig and sheep market. A large room, however, was labelled *"Pensioners' Armoury"* and three bedrooms were so named. On the ground floor, in addition to space for market stalls there was a small room called a *"Fire Engine house"*, another was an *"Orderly Room"*, alongside a kitchen, living room and a urinal. The elevation with an entrance on to Penkhull Street was much as later photographs show, and another opening was on the plan facing into Friars Street.

Two fish stalls were indicated at the far, lower end of three linked spaces, and 47 butchers' stalls, with 10 places for provision sales and 38 for general merchandise were identified. Places 22 inches wide were allocated for 91 sellers with baskets. What in practice happened is uncertain, although clearly Chapman revised down his proposals of 1836 when he thought twice as many stalls would be used as he found necessary in 1853.[26]

What is uncertain about this Covered Market project, and the earlier ones, is the extent to which traders had pressed for shelter indoors for their stalls, and their willingness to take advantage of new trading conditions. Presumably, the pig and sheep section of the site was in the open, though confirmation of whether this was ever constructed, let alone used, is required. Pride in achievement, however, was displayed a year later, in July 1854, when the opening of the Covered Market was celebrated with a public dinner for those who could afford the tickets.[27]

The effect of offering market traders indoor space was to split them more obviously into three groups. One consisted of those unwilling or unable to pay the price of shelter who thus continued working as previously in the streets. How many there were is unknown but later photographs suggest that they were numerous.

Figure 15: The Covered Market in Penkhull Street with crockery stores and a seedsman's shop either side of the entrance circa 1940

Other sellers had no opportunity to change, for they primarily brought cattle and horses to the market. However, they had available a different way of operating suited to their particular needs. Market conditions for all dealers and customers alike, farmers as well as butchers, could be improved considerably if animal sales took place in a separate dedicated space of sufficient size. Shelter was a secondary consideration. Perhaps the first moves to achieve separation were a consequence of building the Covered Market. The initiative came from an auctioneer.

A uctioneers were well established traders organising sales of crops, animals and equipment in farmyards when, for example, a tenant moved out, or a farmer died and his heir needed to sell up to pay debts. Often, they also advertised an expertise in conducting property and land sales based upon experience and close observation of prices. This brought them trust as guides to building and land values. Nothing is known about any involvement they had in conducting auctions in Newcastle's streets on market days.[28]

In the early 1830s the town had two auctioneers.[29] Both had offices in Ironmarket. William Audley was one, and Thomas Edwards the other. Not an impressive number, as Leek had four and Wolverhampton eight. Neither man can be traced in Newcastle in 1841, and a street search of Ironmarket does not find any auctioneers there.[30] Both advertised their activities in the *Staffordshire Advertiser* in the 1820s. W. & J. Audley for example, on one day in May 1820 ran two auctions, that in the morning in a farmyard at Lane End (Longton) disposed of eight tons of hay, 60 bushels of oats and a cart horse. In the evening, also in Lane End, at the White Lion, Audley sold two dwelling houses, a plot of land and *"a large doubled pew lined with green cloth"* in the north gallery of Stoke Church.[31]

Both firms were still operating in the early 1850s and two others were listed in White's Directory 1851. Messrs Audley & Sons now had an address in Red Lion Square.[32] Messrs Edwards & Sons conducted two very large sales of freehold properties in June 1853, one being land for building in the Higherland area, and the other included cottages in the Holborn and Lower Green districts.[33] The following year, in July 1854, Messrs Audley and Son made arrangements to hold periodic animal and agricultural equipment auctions on the premises of the King's Head Inn on Penkhull Street.[34]

In effect, at more or less the moment that the Covered Market opened, Audley sought to regularise the trade in animals by moving the dealing space to a pub yard and, presumably, out of the street. It may be that this was also an attempt to revitalise cattle sales in Newcastle. The town was not listed in the *Staffordshire Advertiser* as a place with a market that month. Hanley and Stoke cattle markets were to be held twice.[35] Newcastle, in other words, now trailed behind its neighbours as a place where butchers met farmers with cows ready for slaughter. It was probably also the case that Audley's firm had established itself as the principal organisers of animal sales in Newcastle's market. It still had a major role in the 1860s for after the suspension of the cattle market during the plague period, which disrupted previous selling place arrangements, Audley and Findon in November 1868 moved their business to the Sutherland Arms.[36] Thereafter, the firm has not been traced.

Figure 16: The Smithfield Pub Sign rescued for display in the Brampton Museum

It is not known if Messrs Audley and Son acted as an agent for the borough council in market matters. All traders paid tolls on a fixed tariff for the right to do business, and in the case of animal sellers the likelihood is that the fee was determined by the number of beasts brought in. Normally, the Corporation leased out toll collection on an annual basis to an agent making the highest bid. In 1836 a Mr Rhead of Hanley bought the toll rights for £468 which was more than he had paid the previous year. Not that this aspect of market management was an issue causing concern.[37]

By the end of the 1860s, however, animal selling on the streets and pub yards became a matter of controversy. Perhaps the absence of cattle for nearly two years when plague ravaged most farms brought some relief to those who still traded from stalls, waggons and stools in the streets. Ungainly fat bullocks and heifers were not easily controlled, as they were driven along thoroughfares lined by rickety tables and seated old women with baskets of eggs and fruit. The return of frisky beasts leaving trails of dung may not have been universally welcomed. Indeed, the mayor in August 1869 reported that ladies were complaining about access to seller's stalls because cattle blocked their path. Action was required. Some councillors suggested moving animal sales to a dedicated space at Upper Green. Others wanted a Smithfield which, by implication, meant a location away from all streets. There was opposition to both propositions and a dispute about the reputation of Newcastle as a cattle market was evident. One view was that it had already lost its role as a market for fat stock. [38]

A new Cattle Market

For whatever reason, by the last weeks of 1869 Newcastle was convulsed for a fourth time by arguments over improvements to market trading conditions. Reports of two meetings in January 1870 allow a glimpse into the clash of opposing forces on the cattle market problem.[39]

A crowded assembly in the Covered Market on a Wednesday evening, taken to be ratepayers, heard speeches attacking a proposal to shift the sale of cattle from High Street downhill to a field about two hundred yards away. This plan was due to be considered in a Borough Council meeting the following evening. Overwhelming opposition to the move was expressed in a resolution sent to the council objecting to the proposal. The meeting's convenient, sheltered space was, ironically, provided at public expense by the action of town improvers 17 years earlier, after numerous rows about its value.

The following evening 20 of the 24 members of the council engaged in a long, and possibly somewhat heated, debate which the county's principal newspaper reported in detail. Alderman Cartwright put the motion to lease a field offered by the Duke of Sutherland for 99 years, and to spend £500 laying it out with suitable facilities to hold and sell cattle. He argued that people were shocked on market days to find the footpaths impassable and streets blocked by cattle, causing scenes disgusting to behold. The Markets and Fairs Committee had searched for some central position in which to locate a dedicated selling area, but failed. The Duke's offer was the best available site. He also stressed that fat cattle could not be effectively displayed in the current streets because they were subject to battering and damage. These were the most highly prized animals, fed to produce the finest beef and ready for slaughter. They were not brought often enough to the detriment of the market. A recently opened railway line to Market Drayton was potentially a means of accessing Shropshire cattle considered the best of their kind, but decent facilities were required to attract farmers away from other market places. Cartwright noted Hanley as one. He considered £500 to be an affordable cost to the ratepayers.

The need to improve conditions in the animal market was accepted by some councillors, but the cost was considered wrongly calculated and too much, the time for action not yet reached, and the proposed location damaging to pubs, whose country customers would no longer be on their doorsteps. Detailed financial analyses were presented to show predicted annual losses, and allegations were made that council projects in the past had been failures, notably the Covered Market and the public baths. All objections were strongly contested. Attendance at the previous evening's meeting, claimed to be 2,000, was said to be nearer 200, while a substantial number of those with large rate bills submitted a petition in favour of a new cattle market site. The motion was agreed 11 votes to 9, a margin indicative of public division. Twelve months later the new cattle market was in operation.

Friarswood Road Cattle Market – the Smithfield in operation

This new local authority facility required managing to ensure an income, in the first instance to pay interest on the £500 debt incurred in fitting out the enclosure. Cattle and horse selling as a trade was in practice dominated by auctioneers and the obvious agent to run Newcastle's Smithfield was a firm of this kind.[40] As there was a strong view in 1871 that the Covered Market had not been a success, at least from the financial point of view, it might be expected that the operation of the cattle market on the Friarswood site from 1871 would have been closely scrutinised. Success presumably depended on the effectiveness of auctioneers who to all intents and purposes dominated the trade in animals. Municipal improvers would not make progress if another of their schemes was deemed a failure.

By 1872 one auctioneering firm advertised that it had authority to hold cattle sales every Tuesday on the new market ground. It was not based in Newcastle and it is uncertain if it was under contract to the borough council. Messrs Wright and Packer had offices in Cheapside, Hanley, and also in Longton.[41] They are not known to have had dealings in Newcastle prior to this, nor to have been active for long. Messrs Edwards were still trading in the town with sale room premises in Brunswick Street, though not known to be using the cattle market.[42] What is also not certain is whether Wright and Packer had exclusive control of the Friarswood Road sale ground or only had a lease for Tuesdays.

Figure 17: Cattle crowded in Smithfield pens photographed by Clement Wain

By the 1880s monthly cattle fairs were being reported in Newcastle. That in April 1880, for example, had been *'largely attended'* by people tempted out by good weather. There was *'a large stock of cattle'* for sale on the Monday morning, but the horse fair in the afternoon *'was of an average kind.'*[43] In November 1881 *'there were plenty of animals on the ground at an early hour'*, with young stock prominent *'despite shaggy coats from the rough elements, and the running-out in the fields which the animals have had'*. Good weather brought *'a better muster of traders than usual'*. The afternoon horse sale was much larger than usual with many animals of good quality. A good supply of pigs was available, and overall *'activity was much above the average'*.[44]

Market activity can be expected to fluctuate, and a quiet day occasionally was normal. At one market a month, however, Newcastle Council's 1871 investment may not have been paying its way. It is also far from clear which auctioneers did business in the cattle and horse fairs. Nothing of substance was said about any of these matters when a government agent came in April 1889 to inquire into the operation of markets. Not that absence of talk about cattle markets necessarily meant that Newcastle was problem free.

Six   Inquiry into Market Rights and Tolls 1889

An assistant commissioner for the Royal Commission on Market Rights and Tolls spent two hours taking evidence from councillors and borough officials about how their market operated.[45] In essence, the Commission collected facts and local opinion about market trading from dozens of sites throughout England, with a view to assessing the extent to which they were beneficial agents in the national economy. Tunstall and Stafford were other places inspected. The focus in Newcastle was on what occurred in the streets and in the Covered Market which allowed a variety of views to be expressed and some sharp divisions to be revealed. One major split was over the continued existence of street selling which it was argued was to the detriment of traders in the Market Hall. Another was over the number and purpose of Fairs which attracted large, noisy and badly sited mechanical amusement devices occupying the whole of the main thoroughfares for days. These at least were the subjects most fully reported in the local press.

Mr Hague explained the problem with street selling. He had the contract for collecting tolls or fees from traders, obtained five years earlier from the council at an auction. Currently he paid £600 a year to the council for this privilege. His problem was the number of hawkers who clearly walked around the streets on market days, avoiding paying any toll. Two of the indoor stall holders confirmed Hague's assertion that hawking damaged their trade.

From owners of carts Hague collected six pence, although as they had goods for sale retail they were able to undercut prices of similar goods on sale in the Covered Market. He considered this unfair competition and wanted cart owners to be restricted to selling wholesale. Stall holders in the street paid him one shilling per day. Inside the Market Hall fees depended on stall length: two pence per foot. In an upper section stalls were one shilling and six pence. In the meat area butchers paid between two shillings and six pence and three shillings and six pence per day for their place. Butter and egg sellers paid one penny for each basket on show.

Several councillors acknowledged that hawking took business away from stalls in the Covered Market, but had no solution to offer. One thought that townspeople with only produce from their gardens to sell should somehow be given an advantage over traders who came from a distance. The clerk to the magistrates, William Dutton (a lawyer of long experience), stated that all regulations were controlled by the mayor who under the terms of the borough charter was clerk of the markets.

There seems to have been some dissatisfaction with the financial position of the Covered Market, for a plan had been considered to alter floor levels to allow for a basement storage space, the rent of which could have covered costs and brought profit. This had been dropped. Constructing the building in 1853 had cost £6,000 and the debt was still being repaid out of tolls, 36 years on.

The only references to the animal market were that Smithfield, as it was called, was rented from the Duke of Sutherland, cost £800 to set up and tolls were used to repay debt. In addition, Hague complained that horses were still brought into the streets to sell and thus evaded toll charges. For whatever reason, the Assistant Commissioner taking evidence did not inquire further, and since he came on a Saturday he had no chance to see the cattle market in operation. Presumably, there was no unfavourable view locally about arrangements at the Smithfield, or at least, none worth reporting.

Much the most contentious matter was the frequent holding of pleasure fairs. William Dutton, although present as clerk to the borough magistrates, announced himself as representing the Manchester and Liverpool District Banking Company when he submitted that pleasure fairs were highly inconvenient and obnoxious occasions. *"On fair days the streets were a perfect Pandemonium, and people desirous of driving through the town had to go round in order to avoid the shows, swing-boats, and other exhibitions, arranged along both sides of the thoroughfares"*. These were the main roads through the town in which the county council had an interest since the recent Local Government Act. Moreover, *"the noise greatly interfered with business, and the passage of people along the streets was almost impossible"*. One can easily imagine the discomfort of clients in a bank office fearing misunderstanding instructions under a barrage of raucous fairground machinery. Dutton also considered that *" domestic life in the vicinity was completely destroyed by the Bedlam, which was kept up till 11 p.m."* He knew that the mayor could order the transference of fairs to the Smithfield, but did not do so even though the great majority of residents locally wanted this.[46]

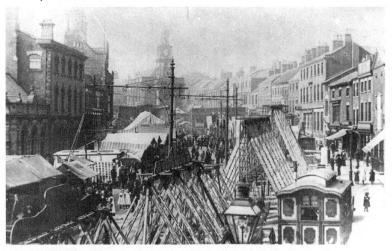

Figure 18: Fair time at Newcastle Wakes 1905

In effect, and Dutton admitted this, the intention behind his attack on pleasure fairs was to secure a change in the law overriding the ancient right to hold fairs on public roads. The Assistant Commissioner appeared to agree that this was a common complaint in many towns and that he was sympathetic to the idea. Councillors were not all allies to Dutton. One alderman thought *"through their attractive character large numbers of people were brought to the town … the fairs were a source of satisfaction to the people"*. Moreover, a municipal election on this very issue had been fought in 1869 and those elected all opposed removing fairs to the Smithfield.

Some sense of personal enmity crept into the exchange, as it was alleged that Mr Dutton might not find satisfaction in fairground music but others did. Dutton reacted by declaring that *"more people were drunk on fair days than on any other day of the year …the fairs attracted a lot of suspicious characters, and it was found that quantities of spurious coin were circulated"*. He was accused of exaggeration, but the

Assistant Commissioner interjected that his critics put trade before the influx of suspicious characters. That was accepted: the interests of trade were paramount. Indeed, Councillor Mellard, a prominent iron merchant, seconded a vote of thanks to the Assistant Commissioner by saying that as one of the largest rate payers he had no objection to fairs in the streets.[47] Not surprising, as he lived well up the Liverpool Road at The Beeches so his nights were not disturbed![48] Photographs of the Wakes Week Fair of 1908 show that nothing had changed.

Seven   Early twentieth century continuity and change

Although it has not been conclusively established, it is possible that a consequence of the visit by the agent of the Royal Commission was a change in Newcastle Corporation's market policy. Management of all three market sites was contracted out to a local businessman, possibly before 1900. A Trade Directory in 1912 recorded that a market was held on three days a week with that on Saturdays principally for the sale of meat, poultry and vegetables. There were butchers in the Covered Market as well as egg and butter sellers, but one section had been taken over for horse sales. The upper floor had offices for unstated purposes. Tolls worth about £700 annually were leased to an auctioneer, George James Heywood, about whom more will be explained later. He was particularly noted as managing the Smithfield also.[49]

Figure 19: Thomas Caddy had this stall in 1908 in addition to his shop on the other side of town

Whatever the date and original terms of Heywood's lease it was renewed in 1916 and was not revisited until 1925.[50] As will be seen later, George James Heywood was an auctioneer who migrated to the town in 1891 from Market Drayton. In respect of market management he was a new broom and decidedly not rooted in Newcastle's burgess traditions. Nevertheless, he did establish a respected position in the town's business circles and its governing body. It is not clear why, around 1924 he attracted criticism for the way he ran the street and Covered Markets after being left a very free hand by the Council's Markets and Fairs Committee. This did not meet frequently. It did decide, however, in August 1925 that when the lease expired at the end of March 1926 it would not be renewed, not even for the five year extension the contract allowed. Briefly, the Markets and Fairs Committee considered that this would open the way to extend the Covered Market into a disused skating rink.[51] Four months later, after council elections and the appointment of a new mayor, the first from the Labour Party, it was agreed not to arrange a new lease but to take the open-air market and that indoors 'in house'. Heywood kept Smithfield; the other markets were to be managed directly by the Borough Council.[52]

In effect, the Markets and Fairs Committee (open for all councillors to attend) had the first three months of 1926 to devise a new management structure, and make those improvements to the material conditions which presumably critics of Heywood's management demanded. Public investment in new facilities was expected to bring greater income to the public purse. A party of councillors visited other local authority run markets; borough officials estimated the cost of buying from Heywood the incandescent gas lamps he had installed in the Covered Market, and the price of replacing them with electric lights; the Surveyor and Chief Constable helped plan a new layout of stalls along Penkhull Street, and advice was obtained from Mr H. A. Wallace, the Market Superintendent for Derby Council. He considered that *"there were great potentialities"* if *"under proper and adequate management".*[53]   G. F. Masefield got the contract for 48 new stalls, but Mr S. C. Moreton, appointed Market Inspector at £250 per annum, found these defective and was dissatisfied with the designs for stalls recommended by Mr Wallace as they were deemed far too heavy and labour intensive to erect.[54]

Moreton was quick to recommend positive action to increase stall rents on Saturdays, rearrange stall locations as more people seemed to browse around one space rather than another, pass new byelaws to prevent the selling of cheap jewellery and quack medicines, and allow 'pitching' only at his discretion. More space was needed for small traders. He found a *"great leakage of people coming to Newcastle and proceeding to Hanley"* to stop which he wanted a new system of traffic control. The Covered Market was a huge fire risk, required a complete overhaul and its offensive lavatory dealt with. His request for the traders to form a committee to liaise with him to keep order was met by the Markets and Fairs Committee asking Councillor Pepper, a man with a stall in the market, to arrange for this.[55] March 31 came and went; the Council took control, and some legal challenge from Heywood was settled, but all was far from ready for a grand reopening.

One significant enhancement of the outdoor market was the provision of electric lights at an estimated cost of £350. The Covered Market had its gas lamps replaced for £35. One issue which distracted attention was a proposal to convert the skating rink into a wholesale market. The lack of such an institution was felt in the Potteries as well as Newcastle, which some saw as a business opportunity for the older borough to seize. Moreton thought the prospects were good, but despite interest from Manchester and Liverpool merchants the idea never materialised. At the Bank Holiday on 2 August the outdoor market was declared open in its new gloriously canopied form.[56] A Friday market was added to Saturday and Monday at the request of some traders.

Not that this remained uncontroversial for long. Something of the undercurrents of dissatisfaction were revealed two years later at a meeting of a newly influential organisation in the borough. It was stated at Newcastle and District Trades and Labour Council in April 1928 that *"the market was now better controlled and directed than when it was in private hands, but it was only when it came directly under the Corporation that the agitation among the traders began to be heard"*.[57] Anthony Moran, the speaker, was in a position to know, as both a Councillor on the Markets and Fairs Committee and as the leading light in the local labour movement. He was not reported as explaining, however, when and why market management had been handed to a private contractor,

George Heywood, in the first instance, or what caused the Council to reduce Heywood's involvement rather than cancel his lease completely.

Clearly, the agitators to whom Moran referred were shopkeepers, particularly those with premises fronting on to the open market space in Penkhull Street. They were united in Newcastle's recently formed Chamber of Trade which adopted resolutions approving the holding of a market in principle, but only if its management was done with consideration to the views of shop owners.[58]   In particular, members of the Chamber demanded *"that more space should be allowed so that private vehicles may have ample means to approach shops and business premises without obstruction from the stallholders"*. They also wanted it to be obligatory for stall holders to display their names and addresses. Thirdly, there was strong objection to three market days – that on Friday was especially disliked.

From newspaper accounts with reference to this controversy it rumbled on for most of 1928. Evidently, there had been some previous dissatisfaction with the private contractor's management of the market, on the part of the very same councillors and shopkeepers who subsequently criticised direct council control. Partly this was to do with the council's annual income from the markets being for some time too small, and the cost of new stalls and making other necessary improvements at Smithfield when the council resumed control. One estimate was that the markets would shortly be net revenue earners, and that at about £100 annual profit a market on Friday was justified, and socially beneficial.[59]   It is also possible to detect a consequence of some wider influences affecting Newcastle's role as a retail centre. The tram network had recently been removed and car owners in ever larger numbers expected to drive their vehicles to shop doors. A transport revolution was underway.

More generally, the effects on Newcastle markets of a world war and economic slumps in the 1920s are difficult to trace. In the absence of domestic refrigeration facilities and given the fluctuations in, and the level of, wages common among the working classes, frequent trips to the Covered Market and resort to street vendors were a necessity for many residents. Meat and vegetables were bought sufficient for two or three days only. By their very nature some street traders were itinerant, though some were of the town. An important group were regular, long term stall holders for whom this was their full-time occupation. Most of them probably worked as individuals or as a family, with a cash turnover supporting a very modest standard of living. Few probably kept business records or diaries, and registers of name and date of attendance in the market if kept by Mr Hague, George Heywood and subsequent officials have not been found.

In 1928, on the other hand, there was some disquiet about the state of affairs on market days. It was not just that shopkeepers felt disadvantaged by stalls too close to their entrances and insufficient parking space for a growing number of motor cars. One prominent men's clothing business owner did a count of market traders on two Mondays and first found 61 and subsequently 63 drapers offering their wares. He considered that "*not fair to the rate-paying drapers of the town*".[60]

Earlier that year, In April 1928, a measure of the depth of feeling about what some perceived as a change in the character of Newcastle's street market was provided by the county newspaper, the *Staffordshire Advertiser*. It had a regular column as 'North Staffordshire Notes and Gossip' which reported on debates in the Council Chamber. One week it revealed that a well-established shopkeeper and alderman expressed the views of his colleagues in the Chamber of Trade amounting to a stinging attack on current Corporation policy. The rule that a ratepayer had first claim on use of a stall over a person from out of town was not being applied. Six market gardeners had recently been turfed out of places they had long held – up to 40 years – to accommodate non-ratepayers. He was quoted as going further. *"Most of the stallholders seemed to be "Sheenies" and Jews and it seemed to him that their own men were being turned out to make room for men who came from they knew not where".* He had counted 49 drapers among them, *"more than all the drapers in the town put together".* The gossip column writer added that the alderman *"confided to me after the meeting that the whole of the cheap drapery trade had been transferred from the shops to the stalls held by men from outside the town who paid no rates and instanced one case of a cheap drapery stall that had been placed right in front of a draper's shop".*

A fellow councillor reinforced the charge that an influx of foreigners had driven out local traders from the market. He didn't think the council had legal right to let stalls to *"such traders as [the Alderman] had referred to"*. Most of them came from Manchester, and there was no doubt that Newcastle-under-Lyme was known in business circles in Manchester as *'Mug's Town'* solely because of the way they threw open their streets to these people. Moreover, a practice the councillor was not familiar with had become a feature of market activity. This was *'pitching'*, or selling by Dutch auction, which involved a lot of shouting *"until late the other night"*. An objection to this was that it threatened to undermine the improvement in shop assistants' working hours, reduced after the Great War. The council were now, the speaker argued, *"doing their best, by their present market policy, to bring long hours for shop assistants back again, because they allowed the market to be open longer than the shops."*[61]

Figure 20: The market in the 1890s before trams were running down Penkhull Street

Whatever the tensions which some thought existed between the interests of shop keepers and stall holders, they were not mutually exclusive groups. Thomas Caddy had shop premises in Marsh Street, but also set up a stall photographed in 1908.

Figure 21: The size of the front section of the Covered Market can be appreciated from this photograph in 1934

In Ironmarket a business better known now as Garners, but first established in Deansgate by Moses Jenkinson's father George in early Victorian times, is remembered as having a stall in the Covered Market in the 1940s.[62] Later, it also used the Smithfield. There it had a shed, as it has been described, where farmers could buy grass seed. Ernest Jenkinson had inherited his florist and garden supplies shop, which had moved to a site just above the Municipal Hall, from his father Moses. However, for 35 years, according to a report on his death in 1935, he had not been a hands-on businessman.[63] He was a burgess and active in the Trust, but not in public life. In practice, the Ironmarket shop became the life's work of Edgar and Annie Garner who lived in Knutton in 1911, but moved into the shop premises and acquired it after Ernest's death. They incorporated the business in 1937 as Garners (Newcastle Staffs) Ltd. Edgar died in 1942 and Annie Garner, recalled now as 'old Mrs Garner', was the one who had the Covered Market stall as an additional sales outlet during the difficult war years. This small glimpse into the lives of those who traded in Newcastle's market is only possible because, after successfully running a seeds merchant business and shop in Merrial Street, Garners moved out to concentrate on its still lively Garden Centre at Silverdale.[64]

During the Second World War, despite the investment in military actions, the needs of a post-war town were not ignored. In September 1943 councillors recorded their hope that a new Covered Market could be built when a larger redevelopment of Penkhull Street took place. Discussions in 1944 and 1945, led to market provision in other towns being investigated to see what could be learned, but thereafter no progress was made. At least the inadequacy of the Victorian building was recognised.[65] A plan to involve Messrs Debenhams in the project evaporated.[66]

Figure 22: Michael Rothenstein's painting of The Lower Market in Newcastle 1943 for a project to portray war-time Britain. © Estate of Michael Rothenstein. All rights reserved, DACS 2023 ©Victoria and Albert Museum, London

Recollections of the late 1950s 67

Up by the top of Friar Street and parallel to it was a wonderful early Victorian covered market with quite an impressive stone-built frontage. A host of vendors rented stalls in there; my father's favourite being Garners, for his WW2 allotment seeds, and similar items for sowing in a then heavily cultivated back garden. Sadly, it was demolished and replaced by a big branch of FW Woolworths.

[The street market] far outshone the covered market for fresh garden produce. Mum was very friendly with a couple from Hinstock (?). The good lady (Winnie Dulson) used to keep some extra special stuff for Betty under the counter, because she knew what sort of produce we relished (damsons especially, coming to mind, nothing beats them for jam). Pottery seconds (some almost unrecognisable as such) half-filled another big stall; the other half definitely the pukka versions. Vendors here had the unusual surname Pass.

All these markets absolutely bustled with activity, when I was a lad and often dragged around them by Mum. Westland's buses could be boarded within 50 yards of the High Street markets and also there stopped a regular service, originating alternately from Stoke or Hanley. I never saw any market whatsoever in the Ironmarket, not being that old!

Figure 23: Market day 1963

One of the signs of a resumption to pre-war customs in 1946 was the return of Pat Collins with his fairground amusements four times a year. These attractions added to the gaiety of the street market and the commercial advantages of open-air trading led councillors to discuss opportunities for holding markets every weekday.[68] There were problems providing electricity for lights in winter, and car parking was another vexed issue which troubled the Markets and Fairs Committee. In the Covered Market a number of traders, presumably long established, showed some dissatisfaction with council provided stalls by offering to pay themselves for various improvements to the sites they occupied. By March 1953 plans for an entirely new facility were under consideration, as ten years earlier using the same location in Penkhull Street and within a larger redevelopment project.[69] It was nearly another ten years before work was completed though the Victorian edifice was demolished in 1961. Space for stalls allocated to traders was found in a basement of the new buildings.[70]

This downgrading of a section of Newcastle's market was a reflection of altered shopping habits and changes in retail practices, as affluence became more evident in post-war Britain. As an underground market it did not prove popular and was closed after only a short time.

Figure 24: An unusual view of the market with stalls crowded in front of the Castle Hotel in 1962

The cattle market, by contrast, had been treated separately. It was paid little attention at the time of the 1889 Inquiry, but was a potentially profitable prospect and a distinct business opportunity with its own way of working.

This became evident before 1925 and brings George Heywood and his family to the centre of the story. He started his career in Newcastle as an auctioneer in 1891 and the history of his firm provides the final chapter in the story of the cattle market's existence. A Market Drayton man, George James Heywood left his employment in Shropshire and set himself up in business in Newcastle aged thirty-two. He did this on the basis of his experience of auctioneering while working for over ten years under a partnership in Market Drayton quite likely to have had clients in North Staffordshire. The firm he founded saw the closing of the cattle market in the 1990s.

Eight   Newcastle cattle market and Heywood & Son

By relocating cattle and horse dealing in 1871 to a specific and dedicated site away from the streets, Newcastle borough was following a trend. In part, this was a response to public health concern about the need to keep streets clean and as free as possible from decaying animal matter. Streets on market days became less hazardous and less cluttered, more pleasing as a shopping experience. Although difficult to demonstrate this could well have been an improvement keepers of permanent shops pressed hard for. A similar move was made in Leek in 1874. Cattle selling in Lichfield had more or less moved out of the city centre by 1869 when Winterton & Bealey started auctioneering on a new site no longer a municipal responsibility. The Smithfield in Newcastle was a local authority initiative, but the manner of its management is obscure until George James Heywood took it on lease. Thereafter, this section of Newcastle's market history is closely related to that of the Heywood family.

George James Heywood was born in Market Drayton in 1859, son of a Sanitary Inspector who still lived in this same place with his family at Spring Cottage in 1881. George, aged 22, was then employed as an auctioneer's clerk by Messrs Green and Pearce, who were a partnership advertising sales in the *Shrewsbury Chronicle* and the *Staffordshire Advertiser* in the early part of the decade.[71] He had three brothers and two sisters.

By 1891, George had a wife, Maria L. Heywood. They had a six-year-old son, George A. Heywood, and three other children, the youngest less than a year old. All were born in Market Drayton.[72] The household and George's income were sufficient to support one 15-year-old female servant living in. Their home at Eaton Villas was out on the Shrewsbury Road which befitted George's status as an auctioneer, possibly by then holding a senior position in a flourishing firm.[73]

Messrs Green and Pearce specialised in agricultural sales, as did the other two auctioneering firms established in Market Drayton before 1889. The town and its rural hinterland may not have been large enough for George to envisage setting himself up there as an independent trader, and he therefore looked for opportunities elsewhere.

He found them in Newcastle-under-Lyme. As there are gaps at key times in the sequence of newspapers available for searching, there is no direct evidence that Heywood was in business there on his own account in 1891. A much later report, however, stated that he came to Newcastle that year and opened an office in his own name.[74] Thereafter, for example on 4 March 1893, the *Staffordshire Advertiser*, the county's weekly newspaper with a special focus on rural communities and their affairs, advertised Geo. J. Heywood organising sales at the Newcastle-under-Lyme March Fair and Prize Horse Sale. There were 70 animals for sale including powerful cart horses, cobs and colts with a number of vehicles also on offer. Apparently, in a sale the previous month, cart horses sold at over 30 shillings above reserve prices, by which it was implied that it was the skill of the auctioneer which created this profit for sellers. Other work Heywood did was at farm site sales, as another advertisement announced cattle, sheep, potatoes and manure he was to auction at a farm at Acton near Whitmore following the death of the farmer. George had his offices in Penkhull Street, the main thoroughfare through the town for traffic heading south towards London.

In other words, George Heywood was sufficiently confident in his abilities, and with good enough contacts, to move out of Market Drayton and open up for business in a larger market centre, adjacent to a major industrial conurbation in opposition to several well-established auction houses, notably Louis Taylor and Charles Butters. Indeed, Butters was in the lead nationally helping to form the Auctioneers' Institute for the United Kingdom in 1889.[75] Such a move implies that Heywood had experience and a reputation in North Staffordshire's commercial world acquired over some time. He was just over 30 years old and still resident in Market Drayton early in 1891. He may well have travelled daily by train from home to office for some years.

The business prospered. In 1894 another newspaper cutting shows the firm dealing in house sales.[76] There were no details of the copyhold and free hold property in Newcastle and Wolstanton then being made available. It is possible, but unlikely, that this was building land rather than domestic dwellings, but again an auction was being arranged. Around the same time more business was done at the railway station in Alsager where a cargo of various types of timber, about 10,000 feet in all, was for sale.

Property dealings were commonly conducted at auctions in the Victorian age. There was as yet no practice of offering houses or commercial premises with an advertised minimum price displayed in windows of High Street offices. General descriptions were placed in newspapers and interested parties invited to apply to auctioneers, or solicitors acting for sellers, to see details printed for that purpose.

For example, in October 1896 Heywood was involved in managing the sale of various buildings in and around Audley.[77] One group of three properties consisted of a six roomed house with associated blacksmith's workshop and a wheelwright's workshop, with two cottages occupied by named tenants. Two detached cottages were also for sale with tenants in place, and thirdly a grocer's shop with a bakehouse was put up for sale. As was usual, a start time was advertised and the event located in a public house – in this case the Boughey Arms Hotel in Audley. It was presumably because of his success in these kinds of sale, perhaps also that he had acquired the lease on Newcastle's market, that Heywood found a house for himself and family before 1901 at Rosemary Villas, a group of substantial homes on the Keele Road out of Newcastle.

The Heywoods still lived in the same house in 1911, but clearly there had been some difficult times after the census had been taken in 1901. Maria Louisa was then 42 years old, but presumably died before 1911 as at census time George's wife was Elizabeth, aged 33. Maria Louisa had given birth to seven children in 15 years, the last, Dennis, in 1900. Two more girls were added to George's family before 1911, one in 1902 and the second in 1905. There is a record of the death of a Maria Louisa Heywood in Newcastle in the period April – June 1905 which suggests that in giving life to Phyllis, Mrs

Heywood more or less kept to her practice of producing a child every two years, but could carry on no longer at the age of 46. George had infants in his family to care for and married a much younger woman fairly soon after. Elizabeth came from Leek and had at least one child with George, called Edwin.

Around 1913 George James moved his family to Stone. He acquired an auctioneering business there, formerly run as Messrs Henry Walters, and took personal charge while leaving his son George Amson Heywood to manage the Newcastle office. Business there was based on the lease George James had taken of the retail and cattle market from Newcastle Corporation. George James had to give up part of this lease in 1926 but, nevertheless, George Amson continued to trade at Smithfield successfully, inheriting the firm when his father died in March 1929. The Stone branch, and an office opened at Norton Bridge, passed to another son, Robert S. Heywood born 1893.[78]

George James Heywood was credited with a reputation as an able businessman with deep knowledge of matters agricultural. He was said to be a fine judge of horses and cattle. He had a partiality for Shire horses and ran a Newcastle Society to encourage their use. He was also very involved with the Staffordshire Agricultural Society and was elected to Newcastle Borough Council during his residence in the town. George James was remembered in an obituary as especially strong in his support of the Red Cross in the Great War. In total, charity auctions he organised raised many hundreds of pounds. On moving to Stone he became closely associated with St Michael's Church where his funeral service was conducted, but he was taken to Newcastle Cemetery for burial.

Elizabeth Heywood, his widow, lived in Kingsfield Oval, Newcastle, in 1939 with Edwin Heywood, born in February 1914, an auctioneer and agricultural valuer. They shared their home with two others, Edward Barnes and Muriel MacMillan.[79]

In 1931 the firm was run by two brothers but advertised as Messrs Heywood and Son and did business in Stone Cattle Market as well as Newcastle. In December 1935 they announced that they had acquired the Smithfield Market at Eccleshall and hoped that trading would continue there successfully under their management.[80] In practice, it seems that Eccleshall business was run out of the Stone office under the care of Robert Heywood.[81] In effect, in the 1930s it was clearly very much a family business, though the degree of integration achieved by George Amson and brother Robert is unknown. George Amson in 1937 was busy enough in Newcastle to engage two apprentice auctioneers for three year's training.[82] About the same time he may have been joined by Edwin his half-brother, but he sent his own son, George William Heywood, to a Shrewsbury auctioneering firm for his pupillage.[83] Clearly then, it was not George James, the founder of the firm, who had to meet the commercial difficulties war brought to cattle markets in the 1940s.

George Amson Heywood

George Amson Heywood was born in 1885 and baptised at St Paul's, Burslem on 21 April 1885, the church wherr his parents were married. He married Catherine Boffey Ball in 1919, the daughter of a farmer, and they had a son, George William Heywood, born 4 January 1921.[84] Catherine was then 29 years old (born 27 February 1892). George Amson was of military service age during the Great War 1914-18 but no record of him volunteering or being conscripted has been found. He presumably continued to live in Keele Road after his father moved to Stone, and in the later 1930s occupied Norton House.[85]

During the 1930s George Amson became actively involved in the politics of the borough of his residence and business. In effect, the Heywood firm ran the town's long established and very busy cattle market. This institution was a major feature of the town's economy until 1932 when a substantial enlargement of the local authority's responsibilities took place. The borough had grown in size to an extent since 1920 with a large new residential estate known as the Westlands. In 1932 Newcastle Borough Council took over the former Urban District of Wolstanton. This was not simply a territorial enlargement but also a major change in the character of the borough. It brought in iron manufacturing and industrial mining, clay quarries and brick works with all their attendant environmental and social characteristics for local politicians to consider. The small market town, home to professional services, retail shopping and the kind of dormitory provision for the middle classes scarce in the adjacent Pottery district, was transformed. A ruling authority of 18 councillors and six aldermen grew in number to 36; those representing the ancient wards of the Victorian borough lost their monopoly on power. This was an opportunity, nevertheless, for the ambitious to enter borough politics and George Heywood took it.

These were not the only influences altering the status of Newcastle's cattle market, which was subject also to wider commercial forces at work in Britain in the 1930s. Motor lorries revolutionised the rural transport network and ways farmers brought animals to market. Imports of foreign foods affected demand for locally produced meat, and high unemployment rates reshaped the labour market. Chains of retail shops with large ranges of branded goods expanded. How far George Amson Heywood was aware of the implications of all the changes going on around him cannot be found, but these were interesting times to take up political ambitions.

Apparently, friends had tried to attract him into municipal government quite some time before 1932, but he had resisted emulating his father. His professional life gave him opportunities to develop interests in various associations of land valuers and estate agents. He was a Freemason (like his father), active in a Friendly Society as well as engaged in the management of Newcastle Golf Club. His charitable inclinations were exemplified by the effort he put into a Newcastle Christmas Dinner Fund. As a former pupil of the old Orme Middle School George Amson was a well-entrenched citizen of an ancient borough undergoing significant alterations in character.[86] He could recall it as a town more dependent on its rural links than engagement with the Potteries industrial district. He witnessed the fierce and successful legal battle fought by Newcastle to prevent a take-over by the City of Stoke-on-Trent 1929-31, which had the result of vastly enlarging the borough by amalgamation with Wolstanton.

This expansion of the borough in 1932 was the occasion of George's election to Newcastle Borough Council representing Ward 3, that of the newly built-up areas of Westlands and Clayton. Immediately, he took the post of Chairman of the Rating and Valuation Committee, hardly surprising given his professional expertise in property valuation necessary to the success of his business. Equally, as might be expected, he was always keen to be involved with the Housing Committee, which oversaw the development of the large Westlands estate of private houses and a neighbouring new council housing estate of rented properties on Poolfield. In 1938,

after re-election in 1935, he was made mayor and subsequently alderman which guaranteed him a place on the council for six years.

This put him in the front rank of Newcastle's municipal leaders and thus made it imperative that he took an active part in the borough's life during wartime. For example, he was chair of the local Red Cross Committee which held a big auction event on his home ground of the Smithfield in May 1943 to raise money. George led by working the

Figure 25: George Amson Heywood as mayor 1938

crowd to sell live cattle, sheep as well as whisky and cigars! Other colleagues in the trade joined in, one selling a cow five times when buyers returned it for resale.[87] Earlier, George had been active appealing for money for an Aid For Greece Fund which he may well have set up himself.[88] At another sale in December for the Penny-a-Week Fund for prisoners of war, George was reported as joint secretary to this Red Cross fund.[89]

On the home front, one issue vexing Newcastle's councillors was whether to allow cinemas to open on Sundays when munitions workers, for instance, had a chance to seek entertainment. George Heywood was among those such as Fanny Deakin who by a very small majority forced this through an argumentative full council meeting at the third time the matter was brought for decision.[90]

With the collapse of Germany and a little later Japan in 1945, the way was opened for a new age, though one with its own tensions and political problems. Newcastle was affected as much as other places, continuing to suffer the immediate effects of wartime regulation of food sales and marketing of farm produce. Messrs Heywood, as agricultural auctioneers and managers of three cattle markets, did not recover their ability to trade in pre-war fashion for nearly ten years. Their other business facilitating the sale of houses and land had never ceased, but disruption in the supply of new homes since 1939, immense difficulties in accessing building materials for new private construction, as well as a major shift in government policy to promote the erection of local authority owned houses in preference to private construction, substantially altered the housing market.

George Amson Heywood rode the various fluctuations in commercial conditions and gained some advantage from his position as an alderman on Newcastle Borough Council. In 1946 there may have been a welcome for Pat Collins and his amusement fair returning, but Alderman Heywood was most concerned about using Smithfield as a location. He succeeded in negotiating a deal by which Collins could have access except on Mondays (traditional market day) in return for the council paying for some surface repairs on the Smithfield. He was, no doubt, also well aware of complaints to the council of poor cleansing facilities because of the inadequate water supply. New, larger diameter pipes were necessary.[91]

George Amson's son, George William, became more engaged in the firm's activities. In 1950 the young man spread his wings and entered the local social world of North Staffordshire's businessmen when he was initiated into the 'Ancient Corporation of Hanley'. This somewhat exclusive dining club had a 167 year history of holding a Venison Feast, with meat traditionally acquired from the Trentham estate of Earl Gower, later Marquis of Stafford and Duke of Sutherland.[92] He was also admitted to Newcastle's Rotary Club in May, perhaps replacing his father who had been a member in the 1930s.[93]

Heywood & Son, as the firm was advertised, held on to its control over the animal market on the Smithfield on the basis of a 21 year lease continually renewed.[94] Their operations were subject to the oversight of the borough's Markets and Fairs Committee.[95] Traditional practices in this particular segment of Newcastle's economy, which brought farmers and their families into town on a regular timetable, were also increasingly subject to changing national legislation aimed at improving animal welfare. It was important that the market achieved attested or disease-free status and adhered to new standards in matters such as safety and hygiene.[96] Commercial conditions altered as the country adjusted in the 1950s to a post-war economic environment. The burdens entailed fell largely on the market lessee, and the costs of improvements in the physical structures and cleansing routines had to be met by the Heywood firm.

Locally, one particular proposal to relieve the town of a long-felt transport bottleneck also affected the cattle market. From at least 1954, and certainly 1959, plans were in hand to build a by-pass for north-south traffic along the A34 designed to lie alongside Smithfield. Through traffic would thus move out of High Street. One issue was access from this to the market for lorries bringing in and taking away live animals. As a result, Heywood's business could potentially suffer disruption at the time when the firm had plans for building

Figure 26: Pig auction in June 1939

alterations to improve site facilities. There was also an ambition to build a permanent office for the firm on Smithfield and move out of premises in the Ironmarket.

Figure 27: Edwin Heywood selling cattle in June 1939

There must have been a degree of optimism that Newcastle would remain a thriving animal market place in the light of the amount of business done. [97] In 1964 a Return to the Ministry of Agriculture and Fisheries recorded annual sales figures at over 18,000 cattle, 15,000 sheep and over 22,000 pigs. In the absence of other figures the trend in sales cannot be traced. Financial records are not available so that the viability of cattle market trading cannot be estimated, although at an annual rent of £800 in 1962, the suspicion must be that Edwin Heywood had confidence that it was worth continuing to take the Smithfield lease. Some benefit to the town of keeping the market was implied when the National Farmers Union in 1959 estimated that some 400 to 500 people regularly attended sales at Smithfield.[98] The by-pass was constructed and a three storey office block at one corner of the Smithfield site was approved.[99]

In 1962 George William Heywood died, presumably after taking over the firm from his father, and this left his uncle

Edwin J. Heywood to hold the reins. Robert Heywood was already separated from the Newcastle business and operating in Stone.[100]   Edwin reorganised senior management late in 1961 by bringing in a partner, Vincent McMillan, an ex-Royal Navy officer and experienced land valuer with a B.Sc. in Estate Management.[101] Both were joined before 1967 by John Stops and Edward T. Vincent.[102] Slightly later, one of George William's sons, David, worked in the firm, but soon left. In 1969 Edwin died and this, in effect, ended the Heywood family connection with the estate agency and auctioneering firm founded in 1891.

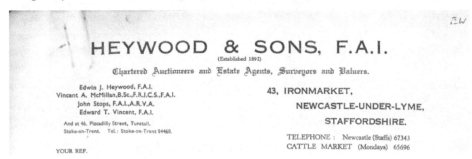

Figure 28 Heywood's letterhead

The cattle market continued to be run by the partnership established by Edwin Heywood which expanded to comprise six Chartered Surveyors with subsidiary offices in Hanley, Leek and Alsager. Indeed, one farmer's son recalls his father having a high regard for Newcastle in the mid-1970s as a place to sell in-calf heifers raised in the Willoughbridge area. As he doubled as a lorry driver taking animals for other farmers to Shrewsbury, Wolverhampton and Market Drayton on days he wasn't travelling to Newcastle he was in a position to judge.[103]   Nevertheless, to those who ran Newcastle's cattle market it was becoming clear that it was in decline.By about 1990 the reduction in farms close to the town as housing estates expanded was compounded by better trading facilities provided at, for example, Uttoxeter and Market Drayton which attracted farmers away from Newcastle. Buyers too went elsewhere. Newcastle's reputation was as a fat stock market dependent on local butchers buying stock and slaughtering at their own retail premises, many of which

Figure 29: Cattle feeding in the Smithfield shed

had closed. The number of local wholesalers also fell. Agents were buying on behalf of national meat trading companies and they were drawn to markets with the largest throughput. Client farmers followed the buyers and it was clear that the future was uncertain and the nature of the trade had changed. In 1991 the century old firm changed accordingly and gave up the lease on Smithfield.[104] The following year the last cattle sales were held and a tradition of well over 800 years of trading animals ended. True to the times, the land was taken over by a supermarket chain of retailers, though the Heywood firm kept one corner for its headquarters. From its windows the last vestiges of Newcastle's ancient street market can be glimpsed on a Monday morning.

Nine   Conclusion

After 850 years of legal trading a market continues to be set up along High Street in Newcastle-under-Lyme. On some days less space is used than was the practice in earlier centuries. The range of items for sale continues to vary, but is more limited than was once the case. Reputedly, Newcastle held a 'market overt' at which goods acquired illegally could be sold, and new owners thus guaranteed rights of possession against subsequent claims. That possibility went some time ago. As this history shows, the attempt to move the market indoors did not succeed, although the effort to make this shift successful was maintained for over 100 years. Dealing in animals was moved entirely away from the streets to a purpose-built site and continued effectively for over a century until commercial forces quite outside the town, and beyond local control, made it unviable. Yet despite this slicing of the market into segments, and only one remaining, there is a strong local perception that Newcastle is a market town and distinctive in character for that reason.

As a weekly, indeed a daily, event held whatever the weather, a street market has considerable attraction for sellers and buyers. Its management is a challenge. Implicit in this account of market activity since 1835, and obvious at certain points, there has been a degree of tension between dealers in goods at temporary booths and shop keepers with premises facing on to the market place and in nearby streets. In early Victorian times this was expressed, in part, as a conflict of interest between burgesses with ancient rights to trade free of toll, or rent, and incomers who did not pay rates to municipal authorities, but were charged a fee according to the size of stall and goods for sale. By the 1920s, shop keepers did not combine as burgesses but as a Chamber of Trade complaining of unfair competition from those 'on the stones'. What changed this situation was the huge expansion of territory administered by the borough council in 1932. By taking over Wolstanton urban district the significance of the market as an element in the borough's economy was reduced.

Coincidental, and with effects less easy to trace and measure, were huge developments in retail trading not fully recognisable until after considerable lapse of time. Among these were the change in means of transporting goods and people. Cars and lorries were obvious witnesses of a transport revolution. Some types of shops have attracted a lot of attention, with the evolution of chain stores from the 1890s onwards, such as Woolworths, Liptons, Home and Colonial Stores and Sainsburys selected as examples. Cooperative Society shops, and very much locally Swettenhams, also multiplied thereby transforming High Street trading.[105] Price has always been a principal point of competition, but quality was another test which market traders had to increasingly face. As against shopkeepers, those with stalls in the market place were less likely to offer goods on credit — 'on tick' as the saying went. More complex ways of branding goods is often picked out as a reason for the success of multiple stores, combining lower prices with quality guarantees. In the two decades between world wars, economic slumps may have created opportunities for open-air traders to counter the pressure of chain store competition. Similar conditions remained available until the later 1950s. By the 1960s an entirely new set of economic forces were shaping the industry of retailing. Proof is to be found in out-of-town supermarkets and shopping malls, plus the ubiquitous ownership of motor vehicles. Currently, debates tend to focus on the effect of low-price multiples and electronic shopping online.

This story of one market space is unbalanced and shallow because the kind of evidence that is required for a more rounded history has not been found. It may not exist. Management is open to public observation and inquiry, trading is not. Neither quantities of goods, their types and prices, nor even the names and addresses of dealers, are in surviving records. Buyers are inevitably anonymous, not known to have left household accounts with a note about purchases in the market. Those aspects of market forces beloved by economists, those iconic laws of supply and demand, simply cannot be investigated at the level of

Newcastle market. Yet contemporary debates about the labour market, the market in futures and the money market, are rooted in an understanding of what has taken place every week 'on the stones', not just in Newcastle but in all the other historic market towns of England.

In the distribution of life's daily necessities, food, clothing, household utensils and cleaning materials, and all manner of small wares including trinkets and toys, street market activity was once the only means. In Britain it has been but one dimension for the last 400 years at least. The physical evidence of a market's existence, however, is more of an empty space than an impressive structure. Booths and stalls are occupied for a day, cleared away very often at night. Theirs is an ephemeral existence. Small wonder then that the history of a market, true certainly in the case of Newcastle, is not often examined. Shops may or may not be architectural delights, but they are continuously visible and in ownership and goods offered appear permanent, not transitory. Even so, their individual and collective history as participants in town life is too often undervalued. This account of the most recent era in Newcastle's market development contributes to a wider history of the economic and social evolution of one of Staffordshire's major urban settlements.

Acknowledgements

Numerous people have freely contributed to the production of this book, by giving encouragement, information and substantial assistance in a variety of ways, and it is with pleasure that I acknowledge them in a random order as Lyn and Oliver Leech, Dr Philip Morgan, Rose Wheat, David Barlow, Dr Christopher Wakeling, Eileen and Alan Chamberlain, Barry Shufflebotham, Dr Ian Bailey, Brian Evans and Martin Whalley. Darren Taylor, Liam and George Smith and Jonathan Hill as market traders and Nick Moore as Market Supervisor helped me understand the way the market operates today. James Sutton is especially thanked for guiding me through some complexities of business history. Friends who meet as North Staffordshire Historians are much appreciated for listening to me try out my early ideas and providing useful financial support. It has been a delight to work with and be supported by Delyth Copp and Clare Griffiths at the Brampton Museum where so much material on which to base the history of Newcastle is conserved. Once again I am grateful to be associated with Roger Bloor at Clayhanger Press and for his meticulous attention to detail. Thanks are also due to Councillor Simon Tagg for accepting this study as a contribution to a celebration of Newcastle-under-Lyme's 850 years existence as a chartered borough.

Whatever the result of all this combined effort, however, my largest debt is to my wife, Anne, whose care and support underlies all.

Census and newspaper searches were conducted using findmypast online facilities.

Newcastle under Lyme Borough Council would like to thank the following 850 partners and sponsors for their support during 2023

Keele University

Staffordshire Community Foundation

Newcastle and Stafford Colleges Group

Aspire Housing

Synectics Solutions

Betley Bonfire

Betley Show

Staffordshire Chamber of Commerce

Sharpe Pritchard LLP

Aaron Bell MP

Anchor Care Homes

Chesterton One Stop Shop

Newcastle under Lyme Business Improvement District

Newcastle under Lyme Conservative Association

Newcastle under Lyme Conservative Group

Options Management

Apedale Heritage Centre

North Staffordshire Historians

Image Sources

All images not otherwise identified are reproduced with permission of Newcastle's Brampton Museum.

Figures 1 and 6 by Paul Anderton.

Figures 2, 3, 4 and 5 were supplied by Nick Moore, Town centre Officer.

Figure 10 Rules of the County of Stafford Association for Protection Against Loss by the Cattle Plague : established September 1865. Wellcome Collection. Public Domain Mark.

Figure 11 Reproduced by courtesy of the Trustees of the William Salt Library.

Figure 22 © Estate of Michael Rothenstein. All rights reserved, DACS 2023 ©Victoria and Albert Museum, London.

Figure 23 by Martin Whalley.

Figures 26 and 27 are by courtesy of the Staffordshire County Museum Service (McCann Collection).

The front cover is a water colour by Reg Haggar held in the Brampton Museum, and the frontispiece illustration by Ray Dodd is with the permission of Lyn Leech.

List of figures

End Notes

[1] W. M. Williams & D. T. Herbert, 'Social Geography of Newcastle under Lyme', *Transactions North Staffordshire Field Club*, Vol. 2, 1962.

[2] *Victoria County History of Staffordshire*, Vol. VIII. (p47) Hereafter VCH.

[3] VCH.

[4] Stephen Matthews, 'The cattle plague in Cheshire 1865-66' in *Northern History*, xxxviii March 2001.

[5] *Staffordshire Advertiser*, 1867 November 9. Hereafter SA.

[6] SA 1835 November 14.

[7] SA 1836 January 2.

[8] SA 1836 January 2.

[9] Alun Davies, *North Staffordshire Royal Infirmary*, (Churnet Valley Books 2006) He was there 1831-48.

[10] SA 1836 December 24, birthday dinner for 300 estate tenants etc Mackenzie responded to a toast noting his connection with the family.

[11] SA 1836 February 20.

[12] SA 1836 March 26.

[13] SA 1836 April 23.

[14] SA 1836 April 23.

[15] SA 1836 September 3.

[16] SA 1847 February 20; February 27; March 13.

[17] SA 1847 April 24.

[18] SA 1847 September 11.

[19] SA 1848 April 1.

[20] J. Ginswick (editor), *Labour and the Poor In England and Wales 1849-51: Letters to the Morning Chronicle* (Cass 1983). The reporter was Angus Bethune Reach who interviewed one of the last hat makers active in the town.

[21] SA 1848 August 5.

[22] Appendix to 2nd Report of Commission of Inquiry into the State of Large Towns and Populous Districts, pp48-9.

[23] SA 16 April 1853. Two years later the militia moved into a purpose-built barracks, see Paul Anderton, *Westlands Stories*, (Clayhanger Press 2022).

[24] SA 1853 May 14.

[25] SA 1853 June 11.

[26] Brampton Museum, Newcastle-under-Lyme, NM 1993. 28. Archive Drawer 7. Hereafter references to the Museum archive as BM.

[27] SA 1854 July 8.

[28] Auctions were long established mechanisms for determining the price of goods as they shortened the time for dealing otherwise required for haggling with separate individual prospective buyers. The difficulty is explaining what advantage there was for a seller to use a professional auctioneer as opposed

to conducting the auction personally. Presumably, the seller paid a fee to the auctioneer. One account has it that in the 1950s at Newcastle's Smithfield the auctioneer on declaring a sale paid the seller instantly, half in cash and half by cheque. The buyer was trusted to pay the auctioneer who thereby took a small risk. Until the seller (or whoever had the cheque on endorsement) cashed it the auctioneer drew interest on cash receipts deposited in a bank.

[29] White, *Directory and Gazetteer of Staffordshire 1834.* Hereafter White.

[30] 1841 census.

[31] SA 1820 May 13.

[32] White 1851.

[33] SA 1853 June 11.

[34] SA 8 July 1854.

[35] SA 1854 July 8.

[36] SA 1868 November 21. Was this on what is now the Aldi site?

[37] SA 1836 September 10. It is possible that by setting up an auction in a pub yard Messrs Audley allowed cattle sellers to avoid paying a toll per animal on the basis that sales did not take place in the street.

[38] SA 1869 August 14.

[39] SA 1870 January 8.

[40] The extent to which animal sellers and auctioneers in Newcastle actively pressed for a Smithfield with all that this entailed is not entirely clear. Nor is it any clearer in wider studies of histories of auctioneering. See 'Livestock Markets: serving the industry for 200 years' in *Agricultural and Horticultural Development Board 2017.* Hereafter A&HDB article. Found online at projectblue.blob.core.windows. net on 10 September 2022. This outline account claims that the first livestock market was established in Hawick in 1817. The implication is that it was run by, if not created by, auctioneers.

[41] SA 1872 March 2; 8 May 1872.

[42] SA 3 July 1872.

[43] *Staffordshire Sentinel* 1880 April 27. Hereafter SS.

[44] SS 1881 November 8.

[45] SS 1889, April 8.

[46] A brief biography of William Henry Dutton can be found in Paul Anderton, *Westlands Stories*, (Clayhanger Press 2022)

[47] Richard Bartlet Mellard, elected mayor November 1889, SS 1889 November 8.

[48] 1891 Census.

[49] Kelly's *Directory of Staffordshire* 1912.

[50] Borough of Newcastle Minutes of Council and Committees, Markets and Fairs Committee 1925, August 1. Volumes of these Minutes are available in the Brampton Museum, Newcastle. Hereafter the Markets and Fairs minutes are noted as M&F.

[51] The skating rink was quite possibly a section of the Covered Market which had fallen out of use. It was borough property leased out for purposes of entertainment. In the 1950s it was remembered as the 'old skating rink' when used as a garage and storage space for council vehicles.

[52] M&F 1925, August 21; December 2.

[53] M&F 1926 February 22; March 1.

[54] M&F, 1926 March 29; May 19

[55] M&F, May 19, 28.

[56] M&F, 1926 June 25.

[57] SS 1928 April 11.

[58] Chamber of Trade formed in 1927 and held its first annual dinner in 1928. SS 1928 February 3. Its views on the market were publicised in SS 1928 May 10.

[59] SS1928 April 11. Councillor Hodgkinson speaking at the Trades and Labour Council.

[60] SS 1928 September 22.

[61] SA 1928 April 7. I owe this reference to, and thank, Mervyn Edwards.

[62] White 1851 for reference to George Jenkinson as a gardener and seedsman in Deansgate. Confirmed by census entries.

[63] SS 1935 December 27.

[64] Information from David Barlow who kindly allowed financial and personal records of his family's business to be consulted. Annie Garner died in January 1966 as recorded in the Sentinel. She has not been found as a Jenkinson in any census or parish record, but is assumed to have married Edgar Garner about 1902.

[65] NM T5120 Ald2.47.9: 1943 September 21; 1944 February 18; 1945 March 5; 1945 June 22. Hereafter references starting with NM are deposited in the Brampton Museum, Newcastle.

[66] NM T5120 Ald2.47.9; 1945 November 20.

[67] Correspondence with Martin Whalley, who is acknowledged with gratitude.

[68] NM T5120 Ald2.47.9: 1947 February 18.

[69] NM T5120 Ald2.47.9: 1953 March 24.

[70] NM T5120 Ald2.47.9: 1963 January 2.

[71] SA 1929 April 6.

[72] The birth of George's first child in 1885 suggests a marriage in 1883 or 1884 and must have been the one recorded as taking place at St Paul's in Burslem in May 1884, when a George James Heywood married a Maria Louisa Amson then living in the established Pottery town, but born in Congleton. Confirmation of this seems to be the name of their eldest child as George Amson Heywood, born in 1885, and so fully recorded in the 1911 census as living with his parents. Clearly, George senior travelled about quite a bit, almost certainly going into the Potteries on business.

[73] 1891 Census.

[74] SA 1929 April 6; SS 1938 November 4.

[75] SS 29 August 1889.

[76] SA 14 April 1894.

[77] SA 17 October 1896.

[78] SA 1929 April 6: SS 1938 November 4.

[79] 1939 Register as found using findmypast. Hereafter 1939 Register.

[80] SA 28 December 1935.

[81] SS 1938 November 4.

[82] Staffordshire County Record office, D4452/10/2/1.

[83] SS 1938 November 4.

[84] SS 1938 November 4.

[85] 1939 Register.

[86] SS 1938 November 4; 1939 December 14.

[87] SS 4 May 1943 with photograph of George.

[88] SS 12 February 1943.

[89] SS 21 December 1943.

[90] SS 4 February 1943.

[91] NM T5120 Ald2.47.9; 1945 October 16. Inadequate water supply was a long running issue in the early 1950s.

[92] SS 1950 December 1.

[93] SS 1950 May 8: 1938 November 4.

[94] NM T5120 Ald2.47.9, 1946 May 21. It was renewed in June 1948.

[95] NM 2012.27.2 correspondence file 1959-1967, items not separately numbered.

[96] NM T5120 Ald2.47.9; 1953 February 24.

[97] There were still 550 livestock markets in England alone in 1963, A&HDB article.

[98] NM 2012.27.2 correspondence file 1959-1967, items not separately numbered.

[99] Only two were built.

[100] NM T5120 Ald2.47.9.

[101] NM T5120 Ald2.47.9. He has not been found to have been a relation to the Muriel Macmillan who had lived with Edwin and his widowed mother in Kingsfield Oval in 1939.

[102] NM 2012.27.2 correspondence file 1959-1967, items not separately numbered.

[103] Interview with Brian Evans August 2022 remembering accompanying his father while working on the farm during school holidays.

[104] The lease was presumably up for renewal in 1990.

[105] Ian Bailey, *Swettenhams: A North Staffordshire retail business* (Audley and Family History Society, 2023)

Cover Design by Clayhanger Press

Typesetting and Design Roger Bloor

Copy Editor Sara Levy

www.clayhangerpress.co.uk

Printed in Great Britain
by Amazon

30784217R00051